The SUPREME QUEST

Your search for the Truth
Ends there where you are...

The Truth has never been attained through seeking.
And yet, only seekers have attained it.

The SUPREME QUEST

Your search for the Truth
Ends there where you are...

SIRSHREE

New Age Books

THE SUPREME QUEST

Published by
NEW AGE BOOKS
A-44, Naraina Industrial Area, Phase-I
New Delhi–110 028 (INDIA)
E-mail: nab@newagebooksindia.com
Website: www.newagebooksindia.com

ISBN: 978-81-7822-366-7

First Edition: Delhi, 2012

Printed and published by
RP Jain for New Age Books
A-44, Naraina Industrial Area
Phase-1, New Delhi 110 028. India

Contents

Foreword		*vii*
Preface: The face of Divinity		*ix*
Part I: Various Approaches to the Quest		
1.	Seeking Happiness is Seeking God	1
2.	The Means of Attaining God	7
3.	The Binoculars to View God	15
Part II: The 7 Stages of Seeking		
4.	Prayer	25
5.	Thirst and Effort	33
6.	Guru	37
7.	Recognizing	45
8.	Eligibility	49
9.	Wisdom	53
10.	Love	65
11.	Destination	73
Part III: The Three-Fold Path		
12.	The Path of Karma	87
13.	The Path of Devotion	101
14.	The Path of Meditation	115
15.	The Path of Introspection	137
Part IV: Face of the Supreme Being		
16.	The Essence of Religion	151
17.	Significance of Worship of Various Deities	189
18.	Seeking Truth in Idols	195

FOREWORD

First, the world witnessed the agricultural revolution, then the industrial revolution, followed by the information revolution; the time has now come for a consciousness revolution. The emergence of a 'global consciousness' is proof of that. The ease with which seekers and non-seekers attain the experience and access the self, and understand the illusory nature of the mind through Sirshree's methods is contributing to this consciousness revolution.

This book reveals the path to attainment of the truth through an understanding of perennial wisdom or *Tejgyan.* We need to find the point of nothingness which is within each and every one of us—the source or the centre of your being. When you access this state, the wisdom that stems from it is called Tejgyan. Tejgyan is the wisdom beyond knowledge and ignorance—the source of all knowledge, a place where nothing is concealed and everything can be seen clearly, a place which leads you to inner peace.

Through his numerous books and discourses, Sirshree imparts Tejgyan. He guides the seeker towards experiencing the truth through an understanding which flows from Tejgyan. And understanding leads you to the final truth—you may call it self-realization or enlightenment or God-realization or by whatever name. This understanding can also be obtained through a 'system for wisdom' that is imparted in the 'Magic of Awakening' retreats organized by the Tej Gyan Foundation, an organization founded by Sirshree. The Foundation helps disseminate Tejgyan.

This book is not biased to any religion or sect. It is meant for mankind at large. Hence the stress is more on understanding what is being said, behind the words. You will find many words that are taken from the Hindi language. Their explanation exists either within the text itself or in footnotes. These words have been used only because their perfect equivalents do not exist in English.

In the text, some words have been added in brackets in order to bring out the meaning relevant to the given context. It has been attempted to accurately represent the content which was originally delivered in the Hindi language. For this reason, at some places there is repetition of sentences as is common in spoken language and at some places the language used in this book may deviate from standard grammatical norms.

For more information about the retreats based on this book or to provide your feedback or seek anwsers to questions, please write to awakening@tejgyan.com

PREFACE

The Face of Divinity

Every Face is the Face of God Alone

A young painter visited a prison. While walking through the passageway of prison cells, he noticed a hideous prisoner. He thought, "If there was a devil, then this is how he would look." The awful picture of this prisoner was etched in his mind even after he returned home. He painted his picture, which to his surprise became very popular and sold well. The painter was encouraged by this success and decided to paint portraits of all kinds of faces. He began his quest for new faces every day.

After many years, a thought occurred to him, 'Why not paint a portrait that can lead the beholder to the experience of God himself! Why not find eyes that would be more beautiful than child's, looking into which one would attain the experience that is beyond the mind! Is there anyone who is gifted with such beautiful eyes?' After a few months of this quest, he did find such a person with a serene face, seated on the banks of a river. When he painted his portrait, he knew it would sell as no painting had ever sold before. Eager to share his happiness, he picked up both the paintings –the latest and that of the prisoner– and approached the person on the riverbank. He said, "I felt peace only after making your portrait. Here it is." The person looked at both the paintings and was astonished. Lost in a feeling of wonder and elation, he began to dance and sing a hymn of praise.

Why have we obtained this body?
Imbued with intelligence, and love of the heart,
The gift of senses, the vitality of breath,
This mind made up of diverse thoughts,
Who is it that has adorned every creature here?
Who is this painter? Indeed, who is this painter!?

The painter couldn't contain himself and asked, "Sir, please tell me, what's making you dance with such joy?" The person disclosed, "Both of these paintings you have made are of the same person. I was the person you'd seen in jail. Behold the divine grace that has been bestowed, for this last painting you've made also is of me." The hideous prisoner had transformed into the divine persona that the painter had sought.

So it is with every living face here. Every face is being sculpted into the immaculate face of God – the ultimate expression of divinity. Some attain it in this lifetime, while others abandon their bodies midway on their journey. However the real quest for everyone is that ultimate face alone, and this quest goes on each and every day, whether one knows it or not.

We seek this face in the form of happiness. Through everything that we think, say, or do, we are constantly seeking happiness. No one would ever say, 'Now that I am happy today, I don't want happiness tomorrow.' When this quest for happiness becomes a conscious seeking, that is when we become 'truth seekers'.

We have all been seekers from the very beginning. We probably may not have consciously known this. Though it may not be so apparent, every seeker has only one quest – for God alone. Is the quest for God possible in today's world? Is such seeking relevant in today's hectic lifestyle and the constant demand for more and more material goods. We complain of a lack of time. We are drawn into several areas of daily life that demand our attention. One may wonder whether God would reveal Himself before us in such a context. The answer is an emphatic 'Yes'. When we pull the reigns of the racing mind with Bright Understanding* the truth is easily revealed.

Let us understand this with the help of an example. Some children like to tie empty cans onto a dog's tail. When the dog sees the can, it tries to bite it. In doing so, it turns around, to snatch it but the can moves further away. The faster it turns, the faster the can spins around. The dog turns around in circles in an effort to grab the can. This sight is very amusing for the children. When the dog gets tired and stops, the can stops right in front of the dog's face. When the dog was chasing furiously, the can was just moving further away. However, as soon as the dog stopped, the can landed right before its face!

We too are running a blind race without stopping to see what's exactly going on. Morning goes by and evening arrives. We go through joys and sorrows; we are praised one moment and slighted in another. This vicious cycle goes on every single day. What are we really seeking? Where can we find the complete and ultimate object of our lifelong quest? Can the ordinary joys of material life give us lasting peace and completeness? Can it ever be found in the external world? Or do we need to seek within? We need to pause and reflect on this. The time has come to break free from this cycle of delusion and attain Bright Understanding* to commence the cycle of our true nature. We need to raise our perspective and see every incident from a bird's eye view to emerge from the shackles of beliefs and pre-conceived notions. We need to pause and see exactly what is going on in our life. Only then does the way out of this blind race become clear.

Our mind consists of two distinct faculties – the 'contrast mind' and the 'intuitive mind'. The contrast mind is the mental faculty that deludes us by constantly comparing,

---

*Bright Understanding: Also known as '*Knowlerience*' – a new term that points to the experiential wisdom that exists beyond thoughts. It is the understanding that is non-conceptual in nature and exists beyond knowledge and ignorance.

judging, and stamping labels on every object, person, event, or situation. This always blocks us from seeing the world for what it really is. The intuitive mind is natural and does not apply any labels of comparison or contrast. It only focuses on doing things in the best possible manner. When we remain watchful and alert during the exploits of the 'contrast mind' and the spontaneity of the 'intuitive mind', we will begin to come out of this vicious cycle.

It is time for a new cycle to begin in our life – the cycle of the intuitive mind that will lead us to lasting happiness, reflecting our true nature. With the beginning of this cycle, the secret that every face is an expression of divinity will be unraveled before us. Is our face expressing divinity, the ultimate happiness? The purpose of this book is to arouse in us the thirst for this quest and to bring to light prevalent misconceptions related to God. Conflicts in the name of God outnumber all the conflicts in any other field. The purpose of this book thus becomes even more significant and assumes greater urgency.

Let us learn the skill of seeking God each and every day! The truth has never been attained through seeking, and yet, ironically only seekers have attained it. Welcome on board this journey of seeking the ultimate truth.

..Sirshree

Part-I
VARIOUS APPROACHES TO THE QUEST

Chapter 1

People ask, 'Why seek God every day?'
We want happiness every day;
We want laughter every day;
Then why not seek God every day?!

Seeking Happiness is Seeking God

Who is this Painter?

When one sets out in quest of success, all his folks encourage him. If he seeks rank and power, people rally behind him. If he endeavors to become an expert in some art or field of activity, his friends and teachers motivate him. People are quick to applaud those who become billionaires. The presidential candidate receives the support of masses except the opposing party. When one contests in the Miss World or Miss Universe pageant, many people flock to cheer her. So much for becoming someone that you are not! But how many would applaud or cheer you if you just want to be the one you truly are. It doesn't sound motivational in a material sense.

Generally, people do not encourage the endeavor to seek the truth as they have no recognition of the very essence of life. Being lost in imaginary notions about God, people just do not feel that this quest is worth pursuing. Whether one seeks God, happiness, or one's own essence, they are different approaches to the same quest. No sooner does one realize that the quest of God is essentially the quest for unconditional happiness, he begins to give it its due importance.

MAKE THE BEST USE OF YOUR LIFETIME

School children are taught how to be more conscious of their time using the analogy of pocket money. They are given 1440 coins every day for their expenses. They spend around 480 coins at the school lab, another 480 in the garden, about 120 coins in the cafeteria and some 120 coins on the playground. Very little remains to be utilized in the classroom, hardly 240 coins!

Though this is a handy way of explaining the importance of time to children, it is indeed relevant in the context of grown-ups as well. The 1440 coins are the minutes in the 24 hours we are gifted each day in this school called Earth. Every morning we wake up, our pockets are filled with the wealth of these precious minutes. Be it man or woman, child, youth, or aged, each one of us is gifted this wealth of time every day. Interestingly very few of us gather a complete view of how we spend our lifetime in this school.

The eight hours that we spend in the school lab is symbolic of the time spent at the workplace. Students spend this time studying for the future. Eight hours spent in the garden represent the time we spend in sleep. Two hours in the school cafeteria is when we have breakfast, lunch, and dinner and freshen up. Two hours on the playground is what we spend on entertainment. We are left with just four hours out of which, we must allot at least some time for the real purpose of life – the quest for God.

As we can see, we are left with less than four hours in a day to pursue our quest for happiness. However, if we observe closely we will find that these remaining hours are lost in anger, conflict, depression, worrying, and wishful imagination.

> *This is like the man who was walking along a riverbank before daybreak, not knowing how to spend his time until sunrise. In the dim light he stumbled upon a bag containing stones. He sat down and started taking the stones out of the bag and throwing them into*

the river one by one. The first rays of the rising sun gave him a shock. He stared at the last stone that was left. What he held in his hand was no ordinary stone, but a gleaming diamond. The bag had been full of diamonds! You can imagine this man's plight. He had simply thrown away so much wealth. Are we too similarly throwing away our precious time?

There comes a moment, when this precious gift of time on Earth comes to an end. It is only at the very end of their life that most people realize that they were living. Many do not come to know the purpose of life on Earth. Many go through their entire life being caught up in various false and limiting beliefs. They die with these beliefs without knowing the truth. We need to understand some vital truths about life before that moment arrives. We should schedule some period of time at least on a weekly basis to devote to the pursuit of truth. This investment will prove to be of immense worth in our life.

WHY SEEK GOD EVERY DAY ?

People claim that they have been seeking the truth or seeking God since many years. But the question is whether this quest is going on each and every day? Do we remember God only when we're faced with difficulties? If we truly desire to attain the Truth, then the quest for God should relentlessly go on every day. By force of habit, the mind may questions the benefits of spending time everyday for this purpose. We can understand this with the help of an example.

A little girl was pleased to receive a set of four handkerchiefs from her friend on her birthday. However, during her birthday party, these spotless handkerchiefs got stained with paint that was spilled by accident. The little girl felt glum and began to shed tears. A great painter who happened to be in the party went up to the little girl and said, 'Stop crying and

> *bring me a paintbrush.' With just a few strokes of the paintbrush, he transformed the colored stains into pretty flowers, bringing back the smile on the girl's face.*

The question is: Has the greatest painter, who has painted the universe, touched our lives as yet? It requires the touch of this painter to transform the stains that we see in our lives into flowers. For this, the quest for God should be pursued every day. The more sincere and relentless our seeking, the stronger the conviction we will develop that problems come, not to trouble us, but rather to bring us a gift. When our life is touched by the divine painter, all our problems turn into priceless gifts.

You would now appreciate the importance of consistency and perseverance in the quest for God. Let us look at the means of attaining God in the next chapter.

CHAPTER 2

Do not perform good deeds for fear of God.
Love and praise God with a feeling that comes with understanding.
Then good deeds will occur not forcefully out of fear, but spontaneously out of love and admiration.

The means of attaining God

God and Happiness Exist Within

We experience happiness for various reasons in our daily life. It may be the attainment of a coveted position or social reputation. It may also be felt when we receive gifts. However, such happiness only makes us increasingly dependent on external factors. It is very important to be convinced that true and lasting happiness does not exist in external pursuits; rather it exists within us. In fact, whenever we have experienced happiness in life, it has always been due to the momentary glimpse of God, our true innate nature. Isn't this astonishing? Let us understand this with the help of an analogy.

Imagine a wall made of twenty stone blocks, each block representing a particular desire that you want to fulfill. You are standing on one side of this wall and God or the experience of truth is present on the other side. Suppose that one of your strongest desires is to accomplish a given task that you have desperately wanted to complete. When this task is accomplished, the stone block representing this particular desire disappears from its place leaving a gap in the wall. You instantly get a glimpse of God on the other side through this gap, thereby experiencing happiness momentarily. However, since this experience coincided with the accomplishment of the task, you wrongly believe that the happiness was felt due to fulfillment of the desire.

We often hear people say, 'I am happy because I bought a new car... I bought a latest music system.' However, the truth is that no one has ever obtained happiness by acquiring anything in the world. As soon as any desire is fulfilled, the mind becomes vacant momentarily. It is due to this momentary emptiness of the mind that one experiences a few moments of happiness. The block of desire clears for some time and we get a glimpse of God on the other side. This glimpse is the real cause of our happiness.

A brief period after having fulfilled the first desire, a new desire takes its place. Once again, God is veiled as a new stone block replaces the earlier one. At the end of life, one sees that this wall of desires is still intact. New desires have replaced old ones. If there is no end to desires, how can God ever be attained!? If every instance of happiness is due to the momentary experience of God beyond the wall of desires, how can we permanently attain this experience? In truth, we are always in the quest of this experience alone, whether we know it or not.

We need to learn the secret of how to make this wall disappear. Once we unravel this secret, we'll be able to dip into the experience of happiness at will and feel God's presence. Then we need not depend on external pursuits. We need not chase shadows when we are actually in pursuit of light. We only need to build an unshaken conviction in the truth that real happiness can only be found within us; the light that we yearn for is present within us in our true nature.

APPROACHES TO THE QUEST

From the analogy, we could understand that any quest is

essentially the quest for the experience of happiness, the quest for being in the presence of God. Thirst for water can never quench with aerated soft drinks. Until one drinks water one will continue to feel the thirst. This is true with any quest in life.

One needs to identify exactly what is lacking. We are seeking God in and through everything in the external world. Hence, we can re-direct our quest by reminding ourselves 'we are seeking God' whenever we seek something in the external world. From today, whenever you seek happiness, you can repeat the statement, 'I am seeking God.' When you wish like cuddling a child, reiterate, 'I am seeking God.' Whenever you feel like visiting an amusement park or a garden, tell yourself, 'I am seeking God.' If you wish to throw a party, remind yourself, 'I am seeking God.'

Beneath the quest for every kind of happiness, the quest for God is being pursued. By practicing to remember that you are actually seeking God, you will soon find that your attachment to external desires loosens up and begins to dissolve. Every pursuit will then serve as a reminder of your quest for the truth. With this, when every instance of happiness reminds you of God alone, you will soon shift from temporary happiness to permanent happiness.

There are various approaches to the quest for God.

First approach: Quest in ignorance

One who seeks God in ignorance believes that there are many gods. This is known as polytheism, which is more relevant in the Indian context. Those who worship various deities for different reasons are convinced that they should worship Lakshmi (the Goddess of Wealth) if they desire riches. To attain knowledge, worship Saraswati (the Goddess of knowledge). To start a new venture on an auspicious note, appease Lord Ganesha. In this way, all kinds of gods have been imagined. Different deities have been pictured as presiding over different departments, fulfilling different purposes.

People pray to a particular God for something specific that they need. If their desire is not fulfilled, they try another god. It's common to hear people confidently advise, 'If your wish has not been fulfilled, why don't you try visiting the other temple to please that God?" People have such a long list of Gods, that a new God can be worshipped every day! Such a quest happens in ignorance. When people are prepared to come out of such blind beliefs, they begin to progress further. A quest always begins in ignorance and there is nothing wrong about it. The only thing that can go wrong with such a quest is when the seeker stops progressing and remains stuck in ignorance.

Second approach: Quest with knowledge

Those who pursue the quest with knowledge believe that there is only one God. With this approach, one believes, knows, and seeks only the single entity. With this knowledge, there is no seeking for anything else but God. There is no other overriding desire to divert the seeker from the ultimate quest. When one prays with the intention, 'I seek only God, nothing else,' such a quest is backed by knowledge.

When one seeks with such unshaken firmness for the truth, a sense of unconditional acceptance begins to develop. When the quest of God takes place with knowledge, the seeker lives with the understanding that, 'God's will is my will.' Here, even when the seeker cries, the understanding is: 'I am crying only because it is God's will. And given that it is God's will, why not enact His will in full spirit! If I am laughing due to God's will, why not laugh heartily?" With the conviction that everything is happening by divine will, the seeker laughs, cries, and functions by being totally open without any resistance to what comes.

When we lack acceptance, even trivial matters cause a lot of inconvenience to us. We are hassled by petty things in daily life. Whatever we resist persists. When we learn the art of accepting the divine play in everyday life, incidents will cease to trouble us and instead remind us of God. A life led in total acceptance leads to a blissful state, where the best that life can offer gets attracted to you. Hence it has been said, 'There's happiness in acceptance; sorrow in resistance.'

Third approach: Quest in Tejgyan

With *Tejgyan,* the quest for God is already fulfilled. God has already been attained. With the earlier approaches, one renders service with the feeling that God will be attained through such service. But a seeker with *Tejgyan* functions with the understanding: 'God has already been attained and hence I am rendering service. It is not that I will gain happiness through service, but I am rendering service out of happiness. It is not that I will sing hymns so as to attain God. Rather, I sing in the joy of having attained Him. Now there's no burden or stress in the quest for God.'

Let us understand this approach with the help of an example of a father who plays hide-and-seek with his son. The father hides and the child, searches for him. As time passes by, the child begins to get restless and longs to see his father. All of a sudden his father jumps out of a hidden corner and startles the child. Now tears well up in the child's eyes. However, these are tears of joy for having found his father. The child experiences a mixture of emotions – the joy of having found his father, and the shock caused by his father's sudden appearance. After this, the child begins to enjoy the game, since he knows that his father is always available, though invisible. He asks his father to hide again. But this time, there's neither fear nor stress in the seeking. He derives joy in his quest. This is the quest in *Tejgyan.*

We need a special pair of binoculars to seek and experience God. We are already graced with such an instrument – the human body-mind. The human body-mind is essential to seek God as this quest is not possible through any other creature. It appears on the exterior that this is a single body. But the human body has four layers, just like the peels of an onion. Within these layers in the centre resides the formless God.

The four handkerchiefs from the example of the little girl in the previous chapter represent the four layers of the human body which have been stained with our vices. When these handkerchiefs are beautified with the touch of the painter through spiritual practice, they are transformed into a garden of flowers. Due to lack of proper guidance and training, these layers get enveloped with dirt. We shall now clean these four handkerchiefs of the human body-mind by training them.

The four bodies

Instrument for the quest for God - Binoculars

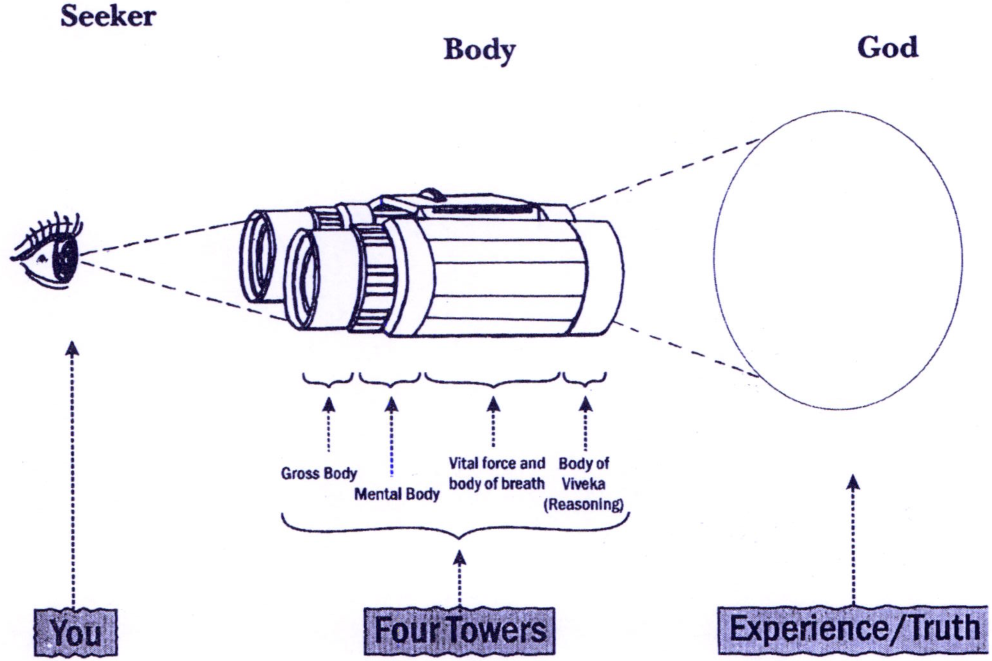

CHAPTER 3

The Binoculars to view God

The Human Body–Mind

Mysterious is the creator of this phenomenal world! The beauty of a painting reflects the beauty of the heart of the painter. The cold of waves reflects the chillness of the ocean. The wise can grasp the whole by knowing just a part. They recognize presence of the ocean by waves.

Is it the eyes that behold the world as forms and colors? Or is someone else peeping through the eyes? Who is the eye of the eyes? This is the mystery that we need to unearth.

Is the world of sound, noise, and music meant for the ears? Are the ears hearing for themselves? Or is someone else hearing through the medium of ears? Who is the ear of the ears? This is a subtle truth that we need to grasp.

Is the nose experiencing the world of fragrance and breath for itself? Or is someone else experiencing fragrance and breath through the medium of the nose? Who is the nose of the nose? This is the secret that we need to know.

Similarly, is the tongue tasting for itself? Or is someone else tasting through the medium of the tongue? Who is the tongue of the tongue? We need to unravel this truth.

Is the skin feeling touch, heat, or cold for itself or is someone else feeling through the medium of the skin? Who is the skin of the skin? This is the riddle that we need to solve.

And finally, does the mind think and feel for itself? Or is someone else thinking through the medium of the mind? Who is the knower of the mind? We need to grasp this subtlety. We need to know and be established in that supreme all-knowing presence.

We have already acquired the instrument required seeking God – our very own body-mind. We need to make use of the four layers of the body-mind to fulfill this quest. In the centre of the body-mind is the fifth, known as *God, Ishwar, Allah,* Self or Witness. Although people have given different names, all these names point to the one truth.

Consider an earthen pot. It is closed from all sides except for its mouth. The pot is useful only because of the empty space within it. You can never fill water if there were no empty space in it! The wall of the pot is the *form* that helps us make use of the space which is *formless.*

Similarly, the formless truth that exists between the four layers of the body-mind needs to be realized. The four layers that become instrumental for this purpose are the gross physical body, the body of breath and vitality, the mental body, and the body of reasoning or wisdom.

It is important to understand these layers and the qualities that affect them because these are instrumental for the quest. Each body has three qualities: *Tamas* – passivity leading to inertia and laziness; *Rajas* – activity leading to restless frantic activity; and *Satva* – equanimity leading to balance and purity.

FIRST LAYER: THE GROSS BODY

This is the grossest of all four bodies – the layer that is given the most attention. The gross body is the physical body, made of food. This body is as important as all the other bodies. This body has a combination of the three qualities of *tamas, rajas,* and *satva* in varying proportion. Among these, the most desirable quality is *satva.*

Tamas (Passive, Lethargic)

A person with predominant *tamas* tends to eat cold, stale and stored food. As a result the body becomes lethargic. At times, such a person also overeats or eats when not hungry, resulting in a gradual increase of *tamas* in the body. Such a person does not like to put in much effort. A person with the tendency of *tamas* likes to sleep for long hours.

Rajas **(Ambitious, Restless)**
A person of *rajas* tendency is an embodiment of ambition, greed and restlessness. They are anxiously engaged in activity all the time to achieve something. Even when they are seated, thoughts of worry and anxiety constantly strom their mind. They are always concerned about what is to be done next. Such people prefer hot and spicy food, which is easy to digest. They often eat less so that they do not get sleep. A person with predominant *rajas* finds it difficult to get to sleep.

Satva **(Balance, Equanimity)**
A person with predominant *satva* eats only in order to maintain normal blood circulation and energy distribution. His food is such that it makes the tongue more sensitive. Such people take a balanced diet and eat only when they are truly hungry. Such people know the art of relaxation. Hence, they can derive joy at work. Just as the heart effortlessly works without stopping, they can remain in poise despite being engaged in the thick of activity.

SECOND LAYER: THE BODY OF BREATH AND VITALITY (*PRANIC* BODY)

The second body is the one consisting of breath. This layer benefits from *Pranayam* (breathing exercises). Dust, smoke, stench, etc. are undesirable for this layer. We cannot underestimate the power of this body. It is this layer of bio-energy that binds the gross and the subtle bodies. It is because of this vital layer that our body-mind functions. This layer determines our lifespan. This layer too has the three qualities of *tamas, rajas,* and *satva.*

Breathing of a person with predominant Tamas
The breathing of such a person is interspersed with frequent sighing. He often draws long heavy breaths and keeps yawning often to compensate for the shortfall in the supply of breath. People often experience lethargy at the sight of such a person.

Breathing of a person with predominant *Rajas*
Such people breathe rapidly. Their breath lacks depth due to frequent activity and tends to be shallow.

Breathing of a person with predominant *Satva*
Such a person does not yawn while breathing; neither is his breath shallow. He breathes normally drawing deep breaths in between thereby using the lungs efficiently. Such breathing always keeps the person balanced due to which there is no need for excess sleep. Such a person feels energetic and can maintain a good balance between work and sleep.

THIRD LAYER: THE MENTAL BODY
This layer represents the mind. Just as a wave can imagine that it is separate from the ocean, similarly the mind also assumes an individual existence of its own, separate from God. When the mind obtains the power of contemplation, it leads to the belief that it is the master. However, the truth is that there is also a witness of the mind. The mind too is being contemplated upon. The mind is not the observer; it is being observed.

On waking up in the morning the world appears before us. The same world disappears when the mind disappears in deep sleep. The waking up of the mind is nothing but the waking up of the numerous topics and tendencies of the mind. This gives rise to attachment, anger and hatred on various topics. The mind gets entangled in the web of the senses.

Whenever the mind associates itself with anything external, the vast variety of worldly manifestation gets created. Imagine what can be created if the mind makes itself the topic of focus! It would be something superior to all external creation. When the mind makes itself the subject of enquiry and contemplation, God is revealed; the mind becomes an instrument for the joy of union with God.

But how can the mind that is so engrossed in the external

world be made to turn inwards? How can it make itself the subject of contemplation? This is the difficulty that a Truth seeker encounters. He can see the world outside, but not the vast expanse that exists within. When man is unable to recognize the presence of God, he begins to imagine God in a limited form. He creates God in his imagination due to which his mind begins to stay within. However beautiful the imagination may be, it is yet only an imagination. In the beginning, this imagination helps to calm the mind, but later, this imagination itself becomes an obstacle in experiencing the Truth.

The mind always divides anything in two. It has the habit of attaching a label of good or bad to any incident. The mental body is always entangled in thoughts. From morning to night, we're always caught up in the web of thoughts. We are always engrossed, either in thoughts of the future or the past. The gap between two thoughts is just not perceived. It is because of this nature of the mental body that dark clouds have shrouded the sun of divinity that shines within us.

> *There was a man who was bothered by his shadow. He thought that he could get rid of it by burying it in a ditch. So he dug a ditch, aligned his shadow in the ditch and covered the ditch instantly. But the very next moment the shadow was in front of him. He tried in vain to bury his shadow several times. In the end he realized that the exercise was futile. He was in a wrong pursuit all the time.*

Similarly people are engaged in suppressing the mind, trying to calm it without understanding. They do not know how to win the mind. The mind can be conquered, not by defeating it, but by making it victorious with the right understanding.

The mental body too possesses the three qualities of *tamas, rajas,* and satva.

A mind with predominant *tamas*

Such a mind seeks credit for whatever is done. It is egoistic and filled with ill-will and hatred.

A mind with predominant *rajas*

A person with the quality of *rajas* keeps his thoughts ever running. With his thoughts, he keeps building imaginary castles in the air. He keeps riding the horses of ambition and beliefs into the past and the future.

A mind with predominant *satva*

Such a mind is spontaneous and natural. Optimistic thoughts always abound in such a mind. A sattvic mind always helps in completing a task with sincerity and concentration. It utilizes the memory and imagination of the intellect to completes a given task at the right time. Such a mind associates with the power to discriminate between the appropriate and the inappropriate, between truth and falsehood.

FOURTH LAYER: THE BODY OF REASONING

The fourth layer is the body of reasoning or the intellect. At its pinnacle, such an intellect which has a sense of goodwill with no trace of deceit attains Bright understanding. The intellect too has three qualities.

Intellect with predominant *tamas*

A person with predominant *tamas* has a corrupt intellect. This intellect is used to spread the fire of hatred. Such an intellect is insensitive and cannot grasp anything subtle.

Intellect with predominant *rajas*

A person with *rajas* has a cunning intellect. Such an intellect is used to deceive people.

Intellect with predominant *satva*

A person with *satva* is clever, but possesses a pure and deceit-free intellect. Such an intellect can grasp very subtle aspects. Such a person does not use his intellect for personal interests, but for the benefit of society.

The experience of God is beyond imagination; it is beyond the capacity of the intellect. The intellect should be used to the maximum to understand its own limitations.

FIFTH LAYER: THE BODY OF BLISS

This body has three principal qualities – Bright happiness, Bright love and Bright silence. Bright happiness is the state that exists beyond joy and sorrow. Bright love is the state of unconditional love that is beyond attachment and hatred. Bright silence is the eternal presence that is the background of both sound and silence. It is this fifth body that desires to experience itself, to know its own nature. This cannot happen as long as we continue to be preoccupied with the remaining four layers.

In the next section we will explore the various stages of the quest, leading to the experience of the fifth – the body of bliss.

Part-II
The 7 Stages of Seeking

CHAPTER 4

If we make it a habit to pray humbly and honestly from the heart, with total concentration and single mindedness, we will begin to see a miraculous transformation in our life.

Prayer

First Stage in the Quest

Prayer is a state, a posture for receiving what God intends to give us. It is the method of communicating with God. Prayer creates a state where we become ready to receive what we need. Prayer is the answer to the question, 'How to get what you want?'

Prayer is the greatest power granted to man even before he encounters a problem. Whenever in crisis, or when troubled by worries, we ought to remember that we have been given a solution even before the problem has occurred. We only need to look for the solution which already lies within you. Prayer helps in bringing out the solution.

Prayer has immense power. Not only can one's desires be fulfilled through prayer; one can even attain the ultimate liberation. Simply surrender your worries to God. Then bring a thought to your mind that God has solved your problem in the best possible manner. This propagates the prayer, to every corner of the universe and creates a way for fulfilling your prayer.

Man's first call for liberation from misery was the beginning of prayer. When a person experiences misery, he begins to think, 'How will this misery end? Is there a power that can end it?' It is these words, these feelings, these thoughts, that take the form of prayer. Some words come forth, some feelings emerg in the form of an intense call from within and the problem is solved. This call is prayer.

PRAYER AND THE QUEST FOR TRUTH

Before any prayer we need to do a Bright Prayer. The Bright prayer increases the potency of our prayer. In the Bright prayer, the seeker says:

> *'Let the prayer which I am now about to say be effective. Let my feeling and intention awaken in this prayer. Let me be able to rightly convey what I want to say in my prayer. Let me be able to inspire my intention, feeling, my thirst and my efforts in the prayer in the right manner. Grant me an understanding of prayer. Let the prayer I am about to say, be for the benefit of all. Let no harm come to anyone due to this prayer.'*

Before we begin the activities of the day, we may say the following prayer:

> *O God! Give me the understanding to recognize what I can change and what I cannot. Give me the strength to change the things that I can and the patience to endure the things that I cannot.*
>
> *O God! Grant me nothing but your love and blessings. For when I receive your love and blessings, other things come automatically.*

In prayer, one can even ask God for God Himself. Let us understand this with the help of a story.

> *There was a king who had three wives. One day, he called all of them and said, 'I need to travel out of the kingdom for around a month. What shall I bring for you on my return? I am very happy with the love you have given me. I want to give you something in return.*

> *There is nothing that can match your love. Even so, I will get you whatever you ask for.'*
>
> *The queens were given a day to make a list of what they wanted. The next day, the queens were called separately to state their wishes.*
>
> *The first queen said, 'I want precious ornaments.'*
>
> *The second queen said, 'I want beautiful costumes from foreign lands.'*
>
> *When the third queen was asked she said, 'O Respected King! I do not wish for material things; neither ornaments nor garments. I only want you. I am asking for you alone. Anything less than you will not satisfy me.'*

The king was extremely pleased with the intention and feeling behind her love. He gave himself to her.

Similarly, if one asks God alone from God, then everything that is His also comes along with Him. If we are asking God for the pleasures and comforts of the world, then we are being satisfied with very little.

Prayer is the first stage in the quest for God. Every seeker of truth is always praying, consciously or unconsciously. Prayer emerges from him when he has to get things which are found wanting. Prayer carries a lot of power. It can work wonders. Prayer can work with just feelings and intention. Words without feeling or intention are ineffective. Yet words are introduced in prayer because they help in bringing about the desired feeling. It is a common experience with many people that initially they were simply reciting words in their prayers without any feelings in them. But later, they noticed that feelings began to emerge with words. Both, words and feelings are essential.

In the quest of God, it is important to understand the significance of prayer. It is from prayer that seeking begins. The seeker calls for guidance. This call itself awakens the power of prayer, increasing the thirst within him. Then the guru finds the seeker, though the seeker may initially feel that he has found the guru.

THE SECRET OF PRAYER

Prayer is the first stage to attaining God's grace. It is only through God's grace that one can understand *maya* (the illusory world) and become detached from it. It is only when the magician wishes that the audience can understand his trick. Similarly, we can understand the supreme magician's trick only when He wills it.

When the fruit of prayer does not come, people respond in different ways. Some may say, 'Perhaps we have not prayed correctly and hence, the results elude us.' Some may simply blame God. Some say that they do not know how to pray. Some say that it was perhaps not in their destiny. Some even think, 'We may not have done enough good in our previous lives and hence our prayers were not heard.' Some may believe, 'God just does not listen to us. He is deaf. Why does he do this only with us? Why has he made some of us rich and some of us poor?'

People have numerous questions, doubts, and complaints about God. They also have ready answers for whatever happens. Some express surprise on obtaining the results of prayer. A popular answer based on prevalent beliefs is: 'You have worked so hard for this! The reward had to come.' And if one does not get the desired results even after working hard, then it will be said that it was not destined to be.

If God would have made everyone rich, then who would work to support you? You would have to do all the work yourself. If everyone was to own businesses and be rich, then who would work for them?' Upon contemplating in this manner, numerous secrets will begin to unfold.

Once, a child was constantly asking his father various gifts. The father too would fulfill all his wishes.

However, he wanted his son to understand the importance of prayer and gratitude. Hence, however trivial a desire his son expressed, he would say, 'Pray to God and then you will get it.'

One day the child asked his father for chocolates. His father said, 'Pray to God and you will get it.' That night, the child prayed and the next morning he found a box of chocolates near his pillow. His father had quietly kept the box when he was asleep.

In this way, the child would get whatever he would pray for. Day by day, the child's faith in prayer increased. He began to thank God every day. Sometimes he would ask for a toy, at times for a bicycle. Since his father knew all his wishes in advance, he would quietly buy them for the child without the child's notice. As the child grew up, his demands increased and so did his faith in prayer.

One day he asked his father for a calculator and prayed. That evening, he happened to notice something that resembled a calculator in his father's shirt pocket. He did not pay much attention to it then. But the biggest surprise for him was when he got the same calculator the next day.

He then realized the secret of how his prayers were being fulfilled. It was his father who was getting the things for him. He was happy that he had finally recognized his father's trick. He was sure that he himself had unraveled the secret. He now knew that his father will no longer be able to trick him. But soon, he understood another secret. It was his father alone who intended that the secret be revealed to him. He had placed the calculator in his shirt pocket with an intention that it should be visible to his son.

Similarly, there are many secrets that we are unaware of. Even when an ordinary magician shows his magic tricks on stage, when he suddenly produces objects out of thin air before us, we are unable to understand the secret of his magic. If we cannot understand the secret of the feats of an ordinary magician unless he wants us to, then how can we understand the divine magic of the greatest magician who has created this phenomenal this world! When we understand this, our prayer will be, 'Kindly shower your grace upon us and reveal the secret of the illusion that you have created.'

This world is an illusion, a game of the great magician. We can understand this only when the great magician wills. Otherwise we lead a life of sorrow and distress assuming this world to be real. When the secret that this world is just an illusion is disclosed, we will not get entangled in it any further. Then life becomes a game – a game of light and shadow, hope and despair, sorrow and happiness, failure and success. If life is truly taken in the spirit of a game, then we will not get entangled in it. Detached from the world, we will lead the life of a witness, a seer. This is possible only when the great magician wants it.

Man often commits a mistake with prayer. When prayers are yet to be fulfilled, he keeps calling for God's grace. But as soon as prayers are fulfilled, he takes credit for their fulfillment. He thinks that his work was accomplished only due to his own effort. As a result, he disregards the power of prayer. Subsequently, when prayers do not get fulfilled, he feels disappointed.

Let us attain wealth, position and glory; but in the bag of detachment. We should be detached from whatever we obtain. Always pray:

> *O God! Let me obtain everything in the bag of detachment.*
> *Let me obtain whatever you have made for me.*
>
> *Let me perform the highest Self Expression through whatever I obtain. Thank you for everything!*

Attachment increases misery. Through inappropriate prayers, man obtains all the wealth he desires in this world, but never attains happiness.

There is a Bright prayer that a seeker offers before any prayer:

O God! What is the Ultimate Truth, I cannot imagine.

I seek to attain that ultimate Truth, the attainment of which the great souls have talked about.

People pray for the attainment of God, and God does reveal Himself. But due to their imaginations about God, they feel God will appear to them just portrayed in movies or on television. Man imagines God in his own image. He believes that God will appear before him wearing a particular form and help him out. Due to this notion, even if God guides him through a neighbor, he is unable to recognize this. Such people seek proof of the fulfillment of prayer according to their own imagination.

Once, a village was devastated by floods. Everyone was running for their lives. There was a devotee who had complete faith and reverence for his God. He began to pray for help. Just then some people who were passing by saw him and offered to extend the support of a rope to the devotee. However, he politely refused, 'Please carry on. My God will rescue me. I have complete faith in Him.'

As time went by, the water level began to rise and reached his waist. His prayers were still on. Just then some people, who were wading through the water in a small boat passed by. They called out to the devotee to join them, but he again refused.

Now the water began to rise rapidly. He climbed on to the terrace of his house. An army contingent that was hovering in a rescue helicopter spotted him. They dropped a ladder towards him. But he remained adamant. In the end, he drowned and died.

After dying, he complained, 'O God! Why didn't you come to my rescue?' God replied, 'I came to rescue you on three occasions; first with a rope, then with a boat, and finally with a ladder. But you did not recognize me. You wanted to see God's help through your own imagination. I was right in front of you, but you refused to recognize me.'

We perceive God through our own imagination. When there is a problem, people pray, 'Now only God can solve this problem.' When someone actually helps them solve the problem, they fail to recognize the hand of God. When we understand this truth, we will not imagine how God will help us; we will always remain receptive and grateful to whatever comes in life.

We have understood the significance of prayer, the first stage in the quest for truth. Prayer prepares us for the quest by raising our receptivity and thirst, and propelling us to undertake the effort for the supreme quest.

CHAPTER **5**

The most beloved is he in whom the desire has arisen – 'I have to listen to the ultimate truth, from wherever possible, at whatever time, beginning here and now.' When the thirst for the truth becomes intense, this thirst gives rise to effort.

Thirst and Effort

Second Stage in the Quest

A woman used to attend truth discourses every evening. One day her husband returned home before she could arrive. Although she had prepared food for him and kept it covered, he could not find it. He waited for his wife to return and serve him food. When she arrived, he scolded her, 'You do not care for me; why didn't you prepare food for me? I am hungry!' The woman replied, 'You did not search properly. I had prepared food for you and kept it covered in this corner.' 'Oh! I did not look in that corner,' remarked the husband. The wife replied, 'Then you must not be hungry.' If indeed he had been hungry, he would have looked in every corner of the kitchen. He was not too hungry and hence sat watching the television while waiting for his wife.

When you return home feeling hungry and food is not served, what do you do? You simply grab a little from the preparation and begin to eat. Do you bother with details of the layout of plates, bowls, spoons or forks? No. You are not concerned about plates and bowls. You simply begin to eat.

But when the seekers of truth begin to receive knowledge, they first want to see how knowledge is being imparted. They would like to see in which plate the knowledge is being served. Whether the language being used is flowery? Is it appealing to the intellect? Is it modern and action oriented? Is it theoretical? Are the verses being recited from the Gita? Is it the knowledge from the Koran? Is something being said from the Bible? They believe that the truth can be attained at a given place, only if it is being served as per their specifications. Otherwise they move onto the next spiritual shop!

In truth, these specifications that seekers expect the knowledge to align with become impediments in the quest. A true discourse of truth is neither for a Hindu, a Muslim, a Christian, or a Jew. It is meant for human beings. People, who attend truth discourses as human beings, without attaching any labels open themselves to attain the experience of the truth. Their thirst is quenched and they feel content.

The knowledge of truth is not directly imparted to the seeker in the beginning. The seeker should first listen to knowledge that awakens the thirst for truth. When the thirst for attaining the truth awakens, the seeker would say, 'Earlier we were not aware of it. We did not know. But now that we know, we cannot afford to wait. We have to attain the truth at any cost.' When the seeker's preparation is such, he does not bother about cosmetics. He is not concerned about the method by which the knowledge is being imparted. He will not be bothered about aspects like the appearance of the guru, the physical age of the guru, his language, etc. When true thirst for the truth awakens, the seeker says, 'I am not concerned whether the plate is made of steel or porcelain. My only focus is on the food – the truth.'

There was a king whose subjects would say, 'O King! We do not get to see you. Kindly bless us with your presence.' One day, the king declared, 'I will meet you all this Sunday at the assembly ground.' All his subjects gathered on the ground on Sunday. The king had organized a carnival with stalls offering a variety of free entertainment and food for all. The king too came and sat in his tent. As everything was being offered free, most people got preoccupied playing games and making merry. Only a few went to meet the king. Earlier, people complained that they could never meet the king. But how many really wanted to meet him? How many were truly thirsty for his sight? We can understand here, how many truly want to attain God? How many have true love and thirst to experience God?

When thirst for the truth intensifies, it translates into effort. In the quest for truth, there is no necessity of physical effort. Physical exercises are necessary for a healthy body. The quest for truth demands the effortless effort of listening to the Truth.

That the thirst for God can awaken to such an extent that only one call emanates from within –

> *Enough! Now only God is wanted. I can rest content only when I attain God. Now, nothing in the world can satisfy me. I have wandered enough behind the pursuits of the world. Worldly pursuits and material objects cannot satisfy my thirst. Now I will be content only when I attain You. Only You can quench my thirst, O God!*

Depending upon the level of thirst for the truth, seekers can be broadly classified into three:

The first kind is those in whom the thirst is intense, due to which they put in efforts to fulfill the quest. This effort is effortless to them. Most people neither have the habit nor the desire to put in efforts. The quality of *tamas* is predominant in most bodies. However, people of the first kind are so thirsty for attaining the truth that when they reach the truth, they become the truth.

The second kind is those people who achieve everything through effort. They always accomplish any decision or resolution they make through ceaseless intense effort. After having achieved everything, they think, 'Now, what is it that still remains to be achieved?' They have achieved everything in the external world through effort. They reach a stage where they think, 'I shall attain God through effort' and their efforts begin in that direction.

Such people do not find it difficult to put in efforts. They perform penance and can torment their own body. They can sit for hours in meditation. Although they are faced with hardships, their willpower is so strong that they withstand everything. Gradually they too begin to understand what effortless effort is. Through the feeling of devotion, effort can easily be put in. In devotion, there is no need of willpower. The truth is attained only when our effort become effortless. When effort is consistently put in, there comes a stage when the effort is given up. It is at this juncture that the truth reveals itself.

The third kind is those with common sense. They contemplate deeply upon profound questions such as – Why have we come to this world? What is the highest attainment? What is the essence of this universe? The Truth that is being talked about since ages must surely have something to it. Their common sense tells them that there is such an experience of truth which is very important to attain.

Those who have common sense know what should be undertaken first in life. What needs to be attended to on top priority before anything else? Where this common sense is lacking, one continues to mechanically do whatever task comes before him. He follows whatever direction anyone leads him to. But once common sense strikes him, the seeker becomes single-pointed. The quest for truth begins to become easy. In reality, the quest for truth is a matter of common sense for the practical intellect.

In our journey till this point, we have come to know that the second stage is about thirst, effort, and common sense. If any of these three has occurred within us, then the thirst to know the truth can awaken within us. When we pray to attain the supreme truth, when we take the first step, effort begins in that direction. Then the quest enters the third stage, when the guru finds us!

CHAPTER 6

There is only one Guru, not thousands.
There can be many body-minds, but the Guru is only one.
God, Guru, and Grace are three names for the same entity.
God is the invisible Truth, Guru is the visible Truth.

Guru

Third Stage in the Quest

In this stage the seeker finds the guru. The guru is the one who has attained the true experience of self-realization and who can direct everyone to attain this state. Only those who know about the ultimate truth can point in the right direction. He alone can tell whether it is easy or difficult to reach there. If someone has not experienced the attainment, how can he even decide whether it is easy or difficult to reach there? Only those who have climbed a mountain can tell you how difficult or easy it is to reach there.

Those who have not experienced the truth for themselves should not be commenting on it. Otherwise, it would become the case of the blind guiding the blind. There are some people who are acclaimed to be knowledgeable, who unknowingly misguide people. They suggest that life can go on nicely even if self-realization were not attained. They make it sound very logical. If everyone is sick, such a sickness will not be considered as sickness. In such a situation, people will not even feel the need for healing. Only those who have got cured will be able to explain the disease and appreciate the need for healing.

In the third stage of the quest, when a seeker is graced with the guru, he progresses further. However, he needs to overcome a major hurdle at this stage. Everyone has a preconceived notion of a guru. Many people commit this mistake in recognizing the true guru. They stick to beliefs such as: the guru must have a particular appearance; he should have renounced the world and should be a avoiding material comforts; he should wear a particular kind of attire; he should use some specific terminology or language; he should perform miracles and provide relief; he should preside over ritualistic practices, the list is endless. If you have any such notions about the guru, then you are not in search of the true guru. You are not truly seeking God. It is essential for you to free yourself from such misconceptions as soon as possible.

The true guru cannot be identified by external miracles. If one wishes that the guru should be able to walk on water, then one can consider a duck as a guru. If one wishes that the guru should fly in the air, then a crow can be the guru. If one can become a guru by abandoning his clothes, then a monkey can become a guru.

The guru stands at the junction of the paths to happiness and sorrow. To people who seek liberation from sorrow, the Guru shows them the road to happiness. Man stumbles on the path of sorrow and the path of happiness appears dark or hazy due to the tears of sorrow in his eyes.

In the beginning, when the guru shows the seeker the path of happiness, the seeker hesitates to walk the path. But he begins to walk the path when he develops complete faith in the guru. By walking on this path, his happiness only keeps increasing and his tears of sorrow begin to vanish. The mist on the road begins to clear as the tears vanish. The road to happiness begins to clearly appear before him. Thus, through the grace of the guru, man attains freedom from the vicious cycle of sorrow and attains the whole and sole purpose of his life.

If you want to be liberated from sorrow, then seek refuge with the one who is free from sorrow. If you seek the truth, then meet the one whose quest for the truth is complete. This is the easiest approach to the quest for God.

IS THE GURU NECESSARY ?

Is it necessary to have a Guru? Is it necessary to have a mother? The answer to both questions is the same. There are children who grow up without parents. However, due to the resulting struggle, they become stonehearted. But those who have had a good upbringing from their parents set a precedent for the world to follow. They appear tough on the outside, but are soft within. They become a source of happiness and guidance for all.

In the external world, we wish for good governance that can make our lives peaceful and productive. We do not want to be troubled by civic issues such as poor infrastructure, lack of good schools, gardens, or hospitals. In the inner world too, strong governance is required to lead a peaceful life. Hence the presence of a Guru in our life is vital. Why does every child go to school and college, when the entire syllabus is available in books? Without teachers to guide us, we will not be educated. In the same way, the presence of the guru is essential for the attainment of wisdom of life.

If the seeker's mind is full of doubts about the guru, then the guru does not proceed with imparting higher knowledge of the ultimate truth. He waits for the seeker to become eligible and receptive to listen to the real truth.

HOW SHOULD THE GURU BE ?

The guru is the one in whose presence the seeker's mind begins to calm down. He is the one in whose presence the exploits of the mind reduce. In his presence, one becomes ready to surrender; the ego becomes ready to bow down. He who frees the seeker from all bondage is the true guru.

The guru rids you of the fear of death and destroys all false and limiting beliefs. The guru is bound to arrive when the disciple is ready to receive knowledge. By having faith in God, one obtains the guru, and by having faith in the guru one attains God.

There is only one guru, not thousands. There can be many bodies, but there is only one guru principle. God, Guru and Grace are different names for the same principle. God is the invisible truth; the guru is the visible truth.

Among the three stages towards self-realization, the final stage is where the Guru is needed the most. The three stages are –

Beginning stage
In the beginning, the thirst for knowing and attaining the Truth is awakened. This thirst can awaken by reading a book or listening to a discourse on the subject. Here at least a beginning is made. There are many seekers who begin the journey, but do not reach the destination.

Middle stage
Here the seeker's thirst for knowledge and the capacity to understand increases. He begins to gain a lot of information and some knowledge. There is a difference between information and knowledge. Information is food for the intellect. Knowledge is that which has been assimilated and becomes functional in the life of the seeker.

Final stage
At this stage, the disciple has understood the truth through his intellect. But he does not yet know the complete truth. The truth has not yet been experienced. But there is a strong possibility here that the disciple mistakes this intellectual understanding to be the attainment of the final truth. He might not continue his journey.

The greatest dilemma for the disciple is at this final stage. It is here that he needs the guru's guidance the most. At this stage, the disciple considers himself to be so knowledgeable that he is not ready to listen further. The disciple could become an intellectual and get tricked by the mind.

Hence the grace of the Guru is vital at this stage. The disciple needs a push from the guru to move beyond the plateau and scale the summit of the quest. If the disciple has complete reverence and faith on the gúru, only then will he honestly abide by the guru's instructions and attain the experience of the truth.

WHO IS AN EFFECTIVE GURU ?

Whom would you call a guru? The Guru is one who is effective. Only an effective guru can impact our life to the extent of transforming it completely. Being effective essentially has two aspects:

1. The complete guru

The complete Guru is the one who is established in the experience of the truth. He is the one who can guide us according to the nature of our body-mind, according to our tendencies and beliefs.

2. Preceptor of current times

The preceptor of current times is the one who knows the need of the times. He knows what kind of delusion people are listening to from all around these days; what they are seeing around them; the conditioning and belief systems prevalent in today's society. The Guru speaks according to this knowledge, giving examples from this context and speaking in contemporary language.

WHO SHOULD BE CALLED THE GURU ?

Should we consider the individual as the guru? Is the guru a body? A body can never be the guru. Most people are trapped in this confusion. They are told, 'This particular individual is your guru. You should not search for any other guru. You should not go to any other spiritual congregation. If you do so, you are committing treachery.' Due to such misleading beliefs, people spend their entire lives in the fear of transgressing.

The true guru is the consciousness within us. It is this revelation of this consciousness that has been called self-realization. This consciousness can also provide guidance through an external body. When the need arises, the guru comes into your life in the form of an external body. If the consciousness wants to reveal itself on its own without external guidance, that too is possible. You could even receive guidance through dreams or intuition.

The consciousness that has not yet revealed itself in the seeker's body, but desires to do so, is the guru. That very consciousness then guides you through another human body, or a book, or through dreams. The seeker should not decide how he would be guided. He just needs to remain receptive.

WHAT DOES THE GURU DO ?

We are like birds that have wings but cannot fly. However, when we see a bird flying, a desire to fly arises in our heart too. So when a person near you attains supreme knowledge, it becomes a great opportunity for you to celebrate, because the doors of supreme possibilities have now opened for you too.

The mere presence of the guru opens up innumerable possibilities for your inner journey. This is because the guru is established in the experience of the Self. The Guru rids you of your habits and tendencies by imparting higher understanding.

A bird has been in a cage for years. Someone now opens the door of the cage to let it free. But the bird clings on to the cage and does not want to come out. After some time, it comes out but still clings to the outer walls of the cage. Now it is necessary for someone to move it away from the cage, give it the final push, so that the bird is able to spread its wings and take flight into the sky.

Similarly, a disciple could get so attached to the words of teachings, that he is unable to grasp the Bright truth beyond those words. A person might understand what the Guru is saying through the intellect. But he may still be deprived of the experience. It is here that the guru watches, gauges, and inflicts the final blow. The guru also sees to it that the words are only taken as a stick that holds the ice candy. Just as you eat candy and throw away the stick, in the same manner after having received Bright Knowledge (knowledge beyond words) one should not remain stuck with words.

IMPORTANCE OF A LIVING GURU AND HIS TEACHINGS

The significance of the living guru is greater because he guides you according to your nature. This speeds up your progress. Whenever you are in his presence, he knows where you are making progress and what is it that limits your progress. The teachings of the living guru have a great influence on the disciple. The guru's words carry power because they emerge from the experience of the truth, from the very source of everything. Hence the disciple listens to him wholeheartedly with a feeling of surrender. He respects and abides by the teachings and instructions of the guru.

> *When the guru comes into the seeker's life, it is the opening up of the highest possibilities for the attainment of the truth. However, there is still another stage that has to be scales – the stage of recognition of the guru's grace. Let us discuss this in the next chapter.*

CHAPTER 7

By the grace of God, we attain the Guru.
By the grace of the Guru, we attain God.
By the grace of both, the individual ego dies.

Recognizing

Fourth Stage in the Quest

Upon obtaining the right guru, if one still does not recognize the guru, then it makes no difference whether one has found the guru or not. We need to be very clear about who is being referred to as the guru. Is it the body, or the one beyond the body? Without this understanding, people are unwilling to listen. They keep saying, 'We have accepted this particular person as our guru since many generations. We go on an annual pilgrimage to perform this ritual in his respect.' One needs to tread the path set by the guru, one needs to walk the guru's talk in everyday life; only then can one attain liberation.

When the truth is being conveyed, we should listen without assuming or drawing inferences. We should stop the self-talk that keeps running in the mind and listen to what is being said 'as it is'. Are we searching for a guru based on notions that we have borrowed from the opinions of people? Then we will never find the real guru. There will be many gurus to guide you. But you will not find the guru who will guide you based on the nature of your own body-mind.

The effective guru will break our tendencies and beliefs, our ignorance and unconsciousness. The effective guru does not boost the individualistic ego in the seeker. There are many so-called gurus who only boost the ego of those who listen to them. People visit many such gurus where they are treated with great respect and felicitated.

At the places where some gurus visit, free public meals are organized for people. The gurus meet everyone, honor and felicitate them. They also visit the homes of some seekers. These seekers swell with pride that the guru visited their home. The seekers then publicize these happenings. In this manner, the ego alone is being publicized. They just do not realize that their ego should have dissolved if the guru were to visit their home. On the contrary, it only became stronger. A true guru will dissolve your ego instead of strengthening it. People fail to understand this as they are not aware of this yardstick to assess the true guru.

Seek the guru with the intention of dissolving your ego. In the presence of the true guru, not everything will happen as per the whims of the seeker's mind. Seekers who yearn for honor and praise may wonder, 'When I was with the other guru, I was honored and respected. Here no one is even noticing me. Why doesn't the guru praise me, despite all my virtues?" The true guru will praise, but only after the final stage of the quest!

Let us obtain the guru and let us also recognize him. Real progress begins only after recognizing the guru. You will then be able to listen to the truth, however illogical it may sound. The truth is beyond the logical constructs of our rational mind. Hence one needs to be first prepared to listen to it. Whenever something that appears illogical is stated, the mind is quick to say, 'This cannot be so. It is being exaggerated.' The seeker takes pride in posing complex questions. When the fallacy of the questions is revealed by the guru, the stubborn seeker may reject the answers by saying 'My question was not as bad as it is being made out to be. I asked such a good question.' Such seekers need to first question their own questions.

The guru's statements will sound paradoxical. For

example, on the one hand, it is said that death is an illusion. On the other hand, it is also said that everyone has to die. This appears contradictory. But both the statements are made in different contexts. When it is said that death is an illusion, what is being said is that life alone exists how can life die?! On the other hand when it is said that everyone who is born has to die, it is in the context of the physical body that this is stated.

If you do not recognize the guru, then you will not be able to listen in a sustained manner. The true recognizing of the guru gives rise to reverence. It is due to reverence that a person persists in the quest, listens consistently, contemplates, and progresses towards the supreme goal. Reverence is a combination of faith, respect, and love. There can be love between two friends, but there need not be respect. It is also not essential that you will have faith in the person you respect and believe that all that he will say will always be right. But reverence is such that it encompasses all the three feelings of love, respect, and faith. Due to your reverence for the guru, you will give due importance to his instructions and also put them into practice. It is only when this happens that you truly progress.

The true identity of the philosopher's stone is proved when any metal touched by it turns to gold. In the same way, the true identity of a guru is recognized when transformation and happiness results in the lives of those who come in contact with him. The guru is the one in whose presence your mind begins to calm down. External miracles do not bring about any experience, happiness, or transformation in the life of the seeker.

When the disciple is prepared, the guru invariably arrives in his life. God's grace manifests as the guru. A living guru can guide us at every step. We need to implement all the instructions from the guru, considering them to be the commandments for our life. Lay before him all your shortcomings and seek his guidance to be rid of them. You have to be deceit-free with the guru. Only by being deceit-free with ourselves and the Guru do we become eligible to attain supreme knowledge.

CHAPTER 8

Do not ask if God exists. God alone is.
Find out whether you exist or not.

Eligibility

Fifth Stage in the Quest

The word 'eligibility' here implies the capability or worthiness to receive knowledge. Let us understand this with an example. There are various characters in a play. If you have to select someone to play the character of Rama (the lead character of the Indian epic, Ramayana), then would you select just about anyone? No. You would say, 'Let me first assess whether the person is suitable for playing the role.' For instance, if that person has the habit of stammering while speaking, he cannot be given the role of Rama. You would say, 'First cure his stammering, or look for another person.'

In the same way, the eligibility of a person who has come to receive knowledge is raised through preparation. Those who listen to knowledge without the required eligibility draw their own inferences and go away. Such people not only harm themselves, but also all those to whom they propagate what they have wrongly. They even stop those who were to attend truth discourses. Hence it has been said that one should receive knowledge only when he is prepared and eligible. A person needs to first build eligibility to receive knowledge. Only then should he be imparted the final understanding. Man's eligibility is prepared only when certain habits of the mind are eliminated.

It is extremely important to assess the habits of the mind due to which one is unable to receive knowledge. These habits should be eliminated first and only then should knowledge be imparted, so that it does not get corrupted. Just as milk that is boiled in a dirty vessel gets spoilt, so also does knowledge imparted to an ineligible person do more harm than good.

If a person who approaches the guru for knowledge is filled with ego and deceit, then he is told, 'First become deceit-free. If you are filled with ego, then there will only be debates and arguments.' When people come with a simple straightforward mind, they are able to receive the truth in the right manner.

The eligibility of those who come to attain the truth is assessed to determine whether they really want the truth. This is just like the interview where candidates are posed questions to assess their eligibility to be able to handle the responsibilities of the role. He, who is truly thirsty for the truth, becomes deceit-free the moment he comes in contact with the guru. He becomes eligible. Gradually, his ability to imbibe knowledge keeps increasing. Only then does he attain the true benefit, which is beyond benefit sand losses.

INTEGRITY IN FEELINGS, THOUGHTS, SPEECH, AND ACTION

Deceit is responsible for a fragmented life. A fragmented life is where feelings, thoughts, speech, and actions are not aligned in a single direction. In order to raise our eligibility, for truth, we need to become free from a fragmented way of life and attain integrity. We should only speak what we think, do what we say, and think exactly what we feel. We can experience completness only when there is integrity among all four feelings, thoughts, speech, and action.

Deceit implies either exaggerating, or playing down, or beating around the bush. Man is constantly indulging in deceit in his business, daily transactions, and his family life.

When a shopkeeper needs to sell something, he first quotes a higher price knowing that the customer will bargain.

It is not that man needs to have integrity only where the pursuit of truth is concerned. We need to be deceit-free even in our routine life. If you tell someone that you would be visiting his house the next morning, then ask yourself whether you truly intend to visit him or you said so just for the sake of saying it. Such conduct makes man non-trustworthy.

Just as deceit is seen in the outside world, we also deceive ourselves. We need to become free from both, internal as well as external deceit. For this we need to first be deceit-free with ourselves. We think something, say something else, do yet another thing, and actually intend something totally different. Ask yourself, 'Am I doing that which I have been thinking, do I have the same desire within me that I am conveying through speech?' Someone says, 'I want to go in quest of God.' If you tell him to come for the truth discourses, he will say, 'I do not have the time today.' This only implies that his speech indicates one thing, his action suggests something else, and his desire is something altogether different. First let us be honest and ask ourselves what we really want? Do we really want to walk the path of truth? If the answer is yes then do we have integrity in our feelings, thoughts, speech and actions?

Once one becomes deceit-free and begins to integrate his thoughts, feelings, words, and actions in the direction of the quest for truth, he then becomes eligible to enter the next stage of the quest – the birth of wisdom.

CHAPTER 9

Through the awakening of wisdom,
Maya (delusion) will remind you of God.
Maya, which was deluding you,
will itself become the ladder for attaining God.

Wisdom

Sixth Stage in the Quest

After one becomes eligible, wisdom is born in the seeker. Till now we have understood five stages of the quest. Beginning with prayer, we move forward with thirst and effort. In the third stage the guru comes in our life. In the fourth, the recognizing of the Guru takes place. In the fifth, one becomes eligible and in the sixth, wisdom is born by listening to the truth.

Wisdom does not mean information. People often mistake information to be knowledge. But it is not so. Wisdom or Bright Understanding is attained only at the experiential level. It can also be called 'Knowlerience' – knowledge that is obtained through the experience that is beyond all concepts. People who mistake information for knowledge claim to have wisdom. People also misuse such information to dominate others.

A person who has information drowns to such an extent in his ego that he does not share the information with his neighbor even though the neighbor may be pleading with him. In those moments, the person feels an air of superiority. How can such information be called wisdom! Information which is being considered as knowledge and used only to display onc's mastery cannot be knowledge.

The word *'gyan'* (knowledge) has come from spirituality. But today it is being used routinely in mundane contexts. It also appears in commercial advertisements. Hence the word has lost its significance and authenticity. It has become corrupted. Hence true knowledge, which is beyond knowledge and ignorance, has been given a new term – Tejgyan (Bright Knowledge). Tejgyan is the experience of Self experienced by the Self in and through every experience.

The truth, that man has been seeking of through the ages has been revealed in many ways. Many mediums have been used. The most significant of them have been parables or stories. Many a time, that which cannot be transferred through words, gets transferred through stories. Through stories, the mind is engaged elsewhere, while the wisdom seeps in silently. It does not face any resistance from the conscious mind.

We have heard thousands of stories till today. Every story reveals some aspect of society. It either criticizes man's beliefs or portrays the variety of human relationships. On all these fronts, the story throws light on the foolishness, deceit, or greatness of the human mind.

We are attached to stories. But have we ever listened to our own story in them? If this hasn't happen, then all stories are worthless. And even if we have listened to them, our listening has been incomplete. Every story has a hero, a heroine and a villain. In our own story, we alone are the hero and the villain. We need to eliminate the villain from our story. For this we need to build an army of wisdom.

Every story has a new and unexpected twist. In our own life, this twist is the emergence of wisdom or understanding. Whatever be your path; be it that of chanting or penance, mantra or karma, devotion or meditation, on every path, the last stage before the destination, is that of wisdom alone The stage of wisdom is so deep that if anyone grasps it, then he is liberated from the duality of joy and sorrow, heaven and hell, deeds and destiny, honor and insult, success and failure, birth and death. Only after reaching this stage do we realize that in reality there is no path to be traversed. We have always been standing at the destination. There is no need to set out anywhere in quest of a path. There was no need to put the body through the rigors of penance. We need to simply stabilize in the realization of 'being', the experience of eternal existence through wisdom. This is easy and effortless. Wisdom grants us the inner eye to perceive the truth. The inner eye works differently from the external eyes.

In this majestic creation of the universe, there are amazing sights to behold as far as our vision can stretch. Our eyes get tired trying to figure out the vast expanses of this infinite universe. This creation is never-ending. However, we are not talking about the vision of this external world. We are discussing the vision that enables us to see the world within.

As our perception, so does the world appear to us. The world appears to us according to the color of the spectacles we wear. Through red glasses, the world is bound to appear red. It is through wisdom alone that one is liberated from these spectacles or limited perspectives and see the world for what it truly is.

Wisdom not only liberates us from 'red' spectacles (anger and contempt), but also from all kinds of spectacles (beliefs) of every color (imagination). Some people do free us from red glasses, but instead give us blue or yellow glasses in exchange. For example, they say, 'This is bad; give it up. But this is good; adopt it.' Wisdom frees us from the duality of good and bad. It frees us from relinquishing and adopting. It lifts us above gain and loss. It makes us recognize the real truth and establishes us in Oneness that is beyond all kinds of duality.

Till today many spectacles have been created to purify the vision – the spectacles of chanting and penance, mantras, karma (deeds), dharma (religion or duty), of devotion and meditation. However one can directly attain wisdom by just listening to the truth.

After having used all the spectacles, being rid of all notions, the understanding that awakens in a seeker enables him to see the Truth as it is. Beyond all color and form, beyond all smell and taste, beyond all thought, sound and touch is the truth, which is experienced after the awakening of the ultimate understanding.

There are various meditation techniques in practice. Techniques could relate to the breath or to awakening mystical powers, or may be related to the opening of the third eye where one sees lights of different colors. However at the end, if the final understanding does not arise, then all these practices are futile. Experiences that are felt at the body level only provide temporary happiness to the mind. However, true wisdom that can only be experienced beyond the mind and body, leads to fulfillment.

Wisdom is attained by the grace of the complete guru.There are three things that happen after the complete guru enters the seeker's life leading to the culmination of the quest:

1) Death of the contrast mind

2) Death of beliefs

3) Birth of Wisdom

DEATH OF THE CONTRAST MIND

Everything in the universe – objects, situations, and events are constantly moving and changing against a fixed changeless point of reference. What is this reference point that is always changeless and ever present within us? There is a still all-allowing presence around which everything else revolves. The quest for this reference point is indeed the quest for God. It is to experience this changeless reference that we need to go within ourselves.

When you are deeply engrossed in some work, you say, 'I just didn't realize how six to seven hours passed by.' This happens because your intuitive mind was functional during this time. It is only when the work of the intuitive mind is over that the contrast mind steps in. If you are cooking food, the contrast mind will torment you with questions such as, 'Will the guest like this food?' When the painter is painting, he is doing so with the intuitive mind. His contrast mind peeps in and says, 'Will this painting sell?' The moment such a thought enters into the painter, the painting begins to get spoilt. When you are descending the stairs, you quickly descend them with the help of the intuitive mind. But, if a thought occurs to you, 'Oh! How smoothly am I descending!', things go awry and you either miss a step or stumble. The intuitive mind works wonderfully. When you are driving a car on a speedway, the intuitive mind says, 'I need to safely take this person home' and it focuses on driving safely. But as soon as the contrast mind comes in, trouble begins. It always harps on, 'I', 'me', 'mine', 'my life', 'my success,' 'my failure'. The contrast mind nourishes and sustains the ego. It is the sole cause of unhappiness and pain.

The cycles of the intuitive mind and the contrast mind move in opposite directions. If you set this right, then the natural cycle of the intuitive mind and happiness begins. Happiness manifests when the intuitive mind finishes its work. Only after the death of the contrast mind, does the natural cycle of the intuitive mind and happiness begin. The death of the contrast mind takes place by the grace of the guru. The guru establishes us in our essential nature by imparting wisdom.

Whenever an incident occurs the contrast mind will make us make remarks like, 'Was whatever happened good or bad? Should it have happened? That person shouldn't have done that!' The contrast mind is like a devil's workshop. It keeps judging incidents based on its assumptions and preconceived notions.

This chattering contrast mind needs to fall. It is a law of nature to not retain anything worthless. For instance, the human tail disappeared when it had no role to play as part of evolution. If the contrast mind too is deprived of work, it will fall. Till the time you support it, it will keep tagging labels to everything and tormenting you.

No incident in itself is happy or sad. An incident is just an incident. However, after it has occurred, the contrast mind comes in and either makes it a happy or a sad incident by labeling it. Until you get rid of this contrast mind, you will remain trapped in the vicious cycle of joy and sorrow. The deeper you understand the contrast mind through wisdom, the more you will stop supporting and giving it importance. When it stops getting attention, it will be eliminated.

DEATH OF BELIEFS

There are several beliefs that are engrained into the human psyche through conditioning received in one's childhood from parents, neighbors, school, the workplace, and most importantly the media. When one breaks out of these limiting beliefs, one realizes that life is not as one had believed it to be. We live with so many labels attached to us; labels like, 'I am a man... a woman... a Hindu... a Mohammedan... a doctor... an engineer... etc.' When we break out of such beliefs, we realize, 'I am none among these. I am not even this body, mind, intellect or breath.' The question that arises is, 'Who am I?' When one experientially realizes the answer to this question, one experiences the joy of freedom. When we begin to know ourselves, the real secret begins to reveal itself.

Standing on a platform, we cannot see the entire train. Only the engine and a few compartments are visible. To see the entire train, we would need to see it from a hill at a distance, or from a helicopter. Similarly, we need to attain knowledge by stepping back and creating a distance from ourselves. One cannot attain complete knowledge, remaining in a well. One needs to learn the art of looking from a high altitude. Only then does the death of beliefs occur.

Every person wants to hear the truth according to his own convenience. He has his own notions or beliefs about the Truth. Many believe that one relinquishes his home once self-realization occurs. Also prevalent is the false belief that a self-realized person does not perform his daily chores of life. Whence did this kind of a notion take root? Such beliefs took root because only a few self-realized souls came to the fore. Among them, the name of Buddha is prominent. But the names of those who attained self-realization through the Buddha never came forth to the world. This happened because the work of imparting knowledge to others did not take place through those bodies. They remained working till the end of their lives in the same state that they were in. If one owned a shop, then he continued managing the shop even after attaining self-realization. If one was a family man, he continued looking after his family. It is not necessary to relinquish the world after attaining self-realization. However, this false notion has taken root in the minds of people.

Seeing the lives of people like the Buddha, who became popular, people think their lives too will take the same course after self-realization. This is a false notion. People assume that their lives too will become famous like the Buddha, or that it should become so. If Jesus performed miracles, then we too should perform miracles upon attaining self-realization. This is a wrong belief which should first be dispelled. There were many who continued their previous occupation after attaining wisdom. Many continued to lead the same external social life as they did before, even after attaining wisdom. Looking at them, nobody ever realized that they had attained self-realization. External appearances can never indicate that a total transformation could have taken place within. You cannot even imagine the real truth because knowing the truth is beyond the mind and intellect. Hence, we need to break out of our beliefs to directly know the truth.

BIRTH OF WISDOM

Someone was asked, 'Is the sun more important or the moon?' In his ignorance, he replied, 'The moon is more important. The sun comes out during the day when there is light. But the moon comes out at night when there is a great need for light.' You would have realized here that even to answer a simple question as this, there is a need for understanding.

Wisdom stands for experiential understanding. Knowledge is of two types – knowledge of ordinary books and Bright knowledge. Bright Knowledge is where we study ourselves; in other words, we read our own book based on the nature of our own body-mind. With Bright knowledge, we rise above all fears, such as hell, fate, humiliation, failure and death. True wisdom enables us to convert our tendencies that were dragging us into Maya and deluding us, into ladders for progress. Those thorns which were obstructing us should be made into ladders to reach the flowers.

If you lack wisdom, then many obstacles come your way that you will not be able to surmount. But with wisdom those very obstacles will support you. For example, a man is ascending a path to reach the destination which is very high at the top. All of a sudden someone throws water onto the path and he begins to slide down. He then tries again. Man too is troubled by incidents in his life. But if he has wisdom, he will fill the same water in a bottle to quench his thirst in the further journey. Further in his ascent, if someone begins to throw rocks at him, he will make milestones out of them. This he does to benefit those who are following him. If someone is throwing sticks at him, then he will learn the art of walking on sticks. If rats are let loose, he will make them gnaw at the ropes that bind his legs. Thus, he will turn every obstacle coming his way to his own benefit. The acquiring of this art alone has been called the birth of wisdom.

With the birth of wisdom, *maya* itself will remind you of reality. The very illusion that was deluding you will become the ladder for liberation.

WISDOM AND COMMON SENSE

The mind has been created for the protection of the body. The body has been created for the Self to know itself. Hence protect your body. Understand the body to be the temple of the Self so that the Self experiences itself to the extent possible. The body is the tool of the mind. The mind is the tool of the intellect, and the intellect is the tool of the Self. The tool should never become the master of its owner. The tool should never become the doer of deeds. The Self is revealed only in the surrendering of the body, mind, and intellect. This completely allows the real owner to use the tools. The tools do not act on their own accord. The greatest use of the intellect is when we realize through the intellect that the experience of God is beyond the intellect. No sooner does this realization dawn, the mind begins to become silent and the Self reveals itself.

WISDOM AND THE STRAIGHT TRUTH

We will try to understand this paradoxical topic with a number of analogies and examples. Through understanding, we are gradually trying to point at the simple straight truth. Truth is very simple. There is no need to complicate it.

> *A person once said, 'I made my son drop the habit of biting his nails.' When asked how he managed to do this, he replied, 'I broke his teeth.' Now, is this a simple method? Is it a straight forward method? Understand here that every person works according to his own*

> *understanding. He is solving problems, but not by the straight method.*

You are already where you want to reach. That which you seek is within you.

> *One day, a person loses his pair of spectacles. When he is searching for them, you ask him, 'Where did you search?' He says, "I looked in the drawers and in the closet." Then you ask him, 'Can you see without your spectacles?' He answers, 'No, I just cannot see without them.' You again ask him, 'Did you definitely search in the closet? Did you look in every corner?' He says, 'Yes, I looked thoroughly, very clearly, in every corner. But it was not to be found.' Then you ask him again, 'Where else did you look?' He says, 'Under the bed.' You say, 'There isn't much light under the bed. Could you still see clearly?' He says, 'Did I not tell you? I looked and there was nothing there.'*

All this only means that he is able to see so clearly because he has been wearing the spectacles all the time. To make him feel his spectacles you are asking him questions like, 'Are you sure you could see it clearly?' He keeps saying 'Yes!' And then it suddenly strikes him why you are repeatedly asking him such questions He now notices that the spectacles were on his eyes all the time. This is exactly what happens in the quest for the truth.

Let us understand this with the help of yet another example.

> *You are standing amidst the mountains beside a pond looking into it. Someone asks you, 'What do you see in the pond?' Looking into the pond you say, 'I see the mountains.', 'What else do you see?' You say, 'I can see some birds that are flying.' Now you are told, 'Shift your perspective. Stop seeing what you were seeing and see what you weren't seeing till now.' You say, 'Yes! Now, I can see myself in the water.' On changing your*

> *perspective, you are able to see your own reflection. It was there from the very beginning. But you were looking at everything else other than this. You did not see your own self.*

In the example above, just one word made you return onto yourself – 'Shift'. Till now you considered yourself to be the body-mind. Now be what you truly are. Just one word did such a great job. Look into the eyes of that person who was earlier looking at the mountains, trees and birds. Now he is saying, 'I am.' As soon as he said this, there was a change in his eyes. Absolutely no effort was needed to see himself. Even his neck didn't have to move. Hence it is said that the Truth is very simple. All that is needed is to shift the perspective. Begin to see that which you were not looking at earlier.

Just as the sun gets hidden behind the clouds, our mind obscures the truth and hides it. If someone were to stand with his back to the idol of God in a temple and say, 'Where is the idol? Where is God?', then what would you tell him? 'Please move aside. Only then will the idol be visible.' The mind says, 'Where is the experience of truth? I can't see it.' The mind needs to understand that the mind itself is the obstacle in realizing the truth. The mind needs to move out of the way so that the truth can experience itself. This can happen only when the mind dissolves in the feeling of pure unconditional love. Let us understand more about unconditional love in the next chapter.

Chapter 10

Awaken yourself to such an extent that
before ordaining your destiny,
God should Himself ask you, 'Is your will my will?'

Love

Seventh Stage in the Quest

With the death of the contrast mind and false beliefs, complete devotion towards God and the feeling of total acceptance and surrender easily arise. Let us understand this through the example of a devotee.

There was a poor man called Hariram. He was a devotee of Lord Ganesha. He religiously worshiped Lord Ganesh every day, made his offerings, and only then had his meals. One day he had to go out to a far off town on an errand. He carried some jaggery (whole cane-sugar granules) along with him for his meals. When he felt hungry, as was his practice, he began to look for a temple of Lord Ganesha. But he could not find any as far as his eyes could see. So he made an idol of Lord Ganesha from the jaggery that he had carried as his meal.

However he used up all the jaggery to make the idol and had none left to make his offerings in prayer. So, he took off a piece of jaggery from the idol itself and offered it back to the idol.

The story is meant to illustrate that, what God gave us, was itself offered back to Him. Hence there is nothing that we can offer from our side to God. What is being offered is a part of Him. The one who is offering is also a part of Him. With this understanding, the ego (individual 'I') that considers itself to be separate from God gets eliminated and true love for God takes birth. For the first time, the mind begins to derive happiness from surrendering. The mind stops taking credit for whatever has happened, is happening, or will happen in the future. A faith develops within man that God alone does everything. Man begins to live being a non-doer, and as a result, is released from the bondage of karma.

A feeling of submission arises within the seeker when the ego within him falls. A feeling of acceptance and love for God arises. One begins to understand that the grace that has been bestowed on us is God's grace alone. Hence one can only offer to God what God has provided us with. Surrendering of the ego to God is possible only in love and devotion for God.

'The one who reads the alphabets of 'love' is the one who knows.' – These words were uttered by Saint Kabir from Self Experience. But the meaning for 'love' that people have adopted is completely different. Hence people listen to the quotes of Saint Kabir and draw their own inferences. Holding onto those inferences and entangled in a false notion of love, they waste away their entire lives. Not recognizing true diamonds, they get preoccupied with ordinary stones. The time has now come to realize the true meaning of love.

What are the qualities of God? Many answers can emerge. But the most significant of them would be Love. People of every religion, sect, or civilization, believe that God loves them and forgives all their follies. How did this belief take root in all the belief systems with the same connotation? The only reason is that the qualities of God were expounded only by those who realized the truth. The experience of the truth was the same in all these bodies and hence the same answer emerged from them all.

There is a saying – 'Behave with others as you would want others to behave with you.' The basic understanding behind this teaching was, 'Whatever you do unto others is in truth being done unto yourself.' This is because there is no difference between others and you. The same consciousness resides in all of us. The same power expresses through all of us. However different and separate we may appear externally, but the truth is that, each one of us is in the same internal experience. When this experience becomes prominent in a body, that body begins to understand and live up to the true meaning of Love. Till then, love is used as a weapon saying, 'If you do this for me, I shall like you... Otherwise I don't care.

By this derogatory use of the word 'love', its fragrance has turned foul. The power of love has now become a weakness and its magic has lost its effect. Instead of becoming a prayer, love has fallen to the level of lust. The expression of love is now looked down upon with perversion. The thirst for love, which could have become the cause for supreme happiness, has now become the cause for grief. Instead of being a pleasant cool flame, the flame of love has become the fiery fire of hell. The charm of love has become hollow and lost its significance. The land of love has become the land of business and money. Songs of love have become a source of entertainment for the mind instead of becoming the cause for its surrender. The nectar of love has become the liquor of blind faith and the cause for unconsciousness. The power of love, which could have become a service, has ended up as a selfish motive. The remembrance of love, instead of leading us to the formless, has ended up boosting the ego sense. The experience of love has lost its sense of fulfillment. People crazy in supreme love, are considered to be strange. The taste of love has been entangled in the senses. The voice of love has been suppressed in noise.

If such injustice was meted out to 'love', it was only due to ignorance. Now the time has come to dispel this ignorance. With this purpose alone, a new word has been coined – 'Tej (Bright) Love'. 'Bright' denotes that which is beyond duality. Bright love is beyond both attachment and hatred. One can understand the true depth of Bright love only by becoming Bright love itself. Only after attaining self experience can one fathom the infinite magnificence of Bright love.

You may have read about the great saints who immersed themselves in devotion. Kabir, Nanak, Tukaram, Dnyaneshwar, Eknath, Chaitanya Mahaprabhu, Meera and many others – all of them, were living examples of Bright love and Bright devotion. What is it that they realized that made them dance, sing hymns and give their entire life to service? To realize that, which they realized, should be our goal; not merely imitating what they did externally. Seeing Buddha seated in meditation, disciples think that they too will attain the truth by sitting in meditation. But they do not realize that meditation was the fruit obtained by Buddha after having attained the truth. Buddha expressed the truth that he attained through meditation. Meera expressed the same through dance and others expressed by singing hymns or through service. On attaining knowledge, some went into silence. Tears flowed in some others. When we too are able to attain Bright Truth, attain Bright love and express it, the purpose of our life will be fulfilled.

> *A lover proclaimed to his beloved, 'I am ready to do anything for you.' To this, his beloved put forth a strange request. She asked her lover to pluck the heart of his mother and bring it to her. Intoxicated in this blind love, the boy killed his mother, pulled out her heart and ran to give it to his beloved. On his way when he stumbled he heard a voice from his mother's heart, 'Did you hurt yourself, my child?'*

This story is meant to convey the message that the highest form of love is mother's love. Among all the relations, it is the mother who unconditionally thinks about the wellbeing of her child. Whether the child is good or bad, she keeps showering unconditional love and affection on the child. But, despite this love being pure, it is not yet Bright love.

The mother feels sad when the child gets into the slightest of troubles. In Bright love, there is no sorrow, only compassion. In Bright love, compassion does not emerge from a negative context, but from happiness. Crying for someone else in Bright love does not bring about unhappiness, but rather purifies the mind.

HOW IS BRIGHT LOVE DIFFERENT ?

Ordinary love is directed towards an individual. Bright love is not individualistic; instead it is for one and all. An ordinary lover is happy with very little. A Bright lover is not happy with little, but becomes happiness and love itself. Ordinary love gets agitated when cheated, and becomes revengeful. Bright love shines further when cheated. Even when being crucified, Jesus could say, 'Forgive them O Lord, for they know not what they are doing,' because he was Bright love. The motive behind ordinary love is, 'How am I benefiting?', 'What do I get out of this?' Contrastingly, in Bright love the thoughts that arise are, 'What am I offering others?' or 'What should I be offering to others?' Ordinary love exists with the body and the mind. Bright love exists in the Heart. In ordinary love, there is always a motive to gain something. In Bright love, love in itself is a gift. It is supreme bliss, the very purpose of life. Ordinary love increases or diminishes with the actions of the other person. But Bright love never diminishes. It is always at its peak.

On attaining Bright love or Bright knowledge, a feeling of oneness emerges for all living beings. It is this love that makes us experience ourselves and all others. This experience manifests through songs and poetry, dance, tears of devotion, meditation and eternal silence. Also, all these expressions could take place simultaneously.

What will happen when this Bright love permeates into our life? This Bright love happens to the mind which is within us. It is the mind's love for the truth, the self-witness. When this happens, the mind which was focusing on a multitude of subjects, stops wandering and begins to think on one subject alone. Man will never want to let go of the supreme bliss that he attains due to Bright love. It is Bright love alone that leads to the death of the ego. It is then that the unmanifest, the unexpressed, reveals itself; this is self-realization.

Only after knowing oneself in Bright love, does one realize how everyone is actually united in Oneness. Man realizes this only through experience. The same Experience resides within all of us. When one is established in Bright love, union with God takes place. This alone is the end of the quest of God – the destination.

God is Love

There are many people who believe that God does not love them. They infer that God does not love them when they face troubles, or when such incidents occur due to which they are inconvenienced in life. 'Why doesn't God love me?' Such statements emerge due to ignorance.

The very fact that you are alive and breathing is because God loves you. Man thinks that God loves him only if things are happening according to his wishes. If things do not occur according to his wishes, he feels that he is not being loved.

God is love and love is power. The power of love can bring about the death of the ego. Otherwise the ego emerges again and again. If man did not have the power of love, he would never have been rid of his patterns and wrong habits. It is only through the power of love alone that we can be freed from the patterns, conditioning and bad habits. The power of love is thus of immense significance. Man obtains significant achievements even with ordinary powers. He can save himself from illnesses. If ordinary power can open up such possibilities for man, the power that comes through love for God can enable him to attain the highest possibility self realization. Hence, love has been called the greatest power of man.

When it is said, 'True love is God's greatest quality. Recognize it,' how do we recognize it? What should one do to recognize it? The answer is: 'Become love'. Only when you become love can you truly recognize love. Otherwise recognizing love is not possible. When this begins to happen in you, you will understand divine love.

God's way of loving is different. God's love is unconditional. God is fulfilling the orders given by man. Man has been granted this freedom by God. This implies that it is man who needs to determine what orders to place, because God is going to fulfill them. We need to learn from our previous order and place new orders (prayers). This is God's constant, uninterrupted, unconditional love for us. The one who learns Bright love begins to love love itself and imparts the understanding of love to one and all.

Understand true love

It is necessary to understand true love at the right time. Otherwise people get entangled in false love for so long that one just does not get the opportunity to come out of it.

Love is only obtained by giving. One does not obtain love by trying to acquire it. This appears illogical. But it is the truth. When you begin to give love, you begin to receive it. In their ignorance and foolishness, people nurture the desire of acquiring love. This is only because logic states that anything is obtained only through acquisition. Hence one always thrusts his hand forward to receive. One never extends his hand to give. Such people always feel the deficiency of love.

People nurture feelings in their minds such as, 'Let the other person first do this for me. Only then will I do this work for him.' Due to these feelings, they move further away from divine love. Even after being deprived of love, if they do not realize their mistake, their whole life is wasted. The very purpose for which one comes on earth remains unfulfilled. One did not attain that alone which was required to prepare for further self-expression.

We need to make use of this understanding of true love to emerge out of false notions and open up the possibility of divine love in our life as well as others' whose life we touch.

CHAPTER 11

No one can liberate you, for you are already liberated...
from the very beginning!
The thought of bondage is a myth in itself
freedom from this myth is true liberation.
Your search for the truth ends there, where you already are.

Destination

When we hear words like *'Supreme being'*, *'Allah'*, *'Ishwar'*, *'Parameshwar'* or *'God'*, we associate various notions and beliefs that come from our past conditioning since childhood. All these notions and beliefs about God need to be dispelled, as truth is beyond concepts and belief systems.

There are certain profound questions about the essence of our existence, our life here, and the purpose of all creation that arise in the mind of a seeker of truth. These questions may lack intensity to start with, but there comes a stage in the life of the seeker when these questions gather intensity and thirst. Who am I? Who is God? What is the purpose of life? Who created God? Is all this a dream? What was there before the universe was created? Does God really exist? One can obtain experiential answers to all these questions through guidance by the right guru. However, until we get to hear direct answers to these questions, we can contemplate on the pointers provided below.

DOES GOD EXIST ?

An atheist says, 'God does not exist'; a believer says, 'God exists.' However, both have incomplete knowledge. The truth is: Only God exists. Whether God exists is a wrong question. Suppose someone who is lying down on the bed is asked, 'Are you awake?' If he says yes, you know that he is awake. Even if he says no, it still means that he is awake. Similarly, if one says that God exists, it means God exists. If one says that God does not exist, it still means that God exists. Even to be able to say yes or no, the body has to be enlivened by the presence of God. Only God exists. Who is refuting his existence? It is he alone who refutes his own existence through the medium of a body that is ignorant.

What is God?

A stranger came to visit a kingdom. He began to tell people strange things about God. As this did not turn out well with many people, they took him to the king and complained, 'This person is trying to spread strange and unheard ideas of God.'

When the king asked him for an explanation, he replied, 'I can prove that I am not misleading people.' He called three ministers and gave each of them a packet filled with soil. Then he asked them to describe what was there in the packet.

The first minister said, 'Everything is born from this. The seeds, trees exist in this soil.'

The second minister replied, 'This is everything except water.'

The third minister answered, 'This is something into which everyone has to dissolve and merge one day.'

After listening to their answers, the stranger explained the riddle of the soil, 'You have all seen that even on asking about something as ordinary as soil, we received three different answers. You can then imagine how many different answers people would have about the God that I was describing. Does truth or God change depending on the answers used to describe?'

What is God? Many different answers can be given. For instance, God is nothing, and the world has been created from this nothing, just as the entire forest emerges from a seed. Now break the seed and what do you find inside? Nothing! God too is nothing. But this 'nothing' is not the nothing that our mind imagines. This 'nothing' has the inherent potential for everything. God is the consciousness, the life within us. In truth, God can only be known through experience. God cannot be described in words.

What is the name of God?

The most apt name for God would be 'Nameless Truth'. Either all names are of God alone, or none of them. All forms are his manifestation, or none. Whenever one states the truth, they are essentially remembering the name of God. The mere chanting of the words 'God' or 'Truth' does not equate to the true remembrance of God. It is only when we think the truth that we are truly remembering God.

There is a difference between thinking the truth and thinking *about* the truth. When we read or think upon the stories of Rama, Krishna, or Jesus, then we are thinking *about* the truth. This has nothing to do with thinking the truth. To think the truth is to think the one that 'I' truly am, to be the real 'I'. Thinking the truth and remembering the name of God is to always remember, 'Who is really performing all actions?' in and through every moment of our life.

The recitation of words like 'Rama' or 'Hari' does give rise to the feeling of peace and devotion; however, they are not the true remembrance of the name of God. The truth that was stated even before Rama existed is the name of God. The truth that was uttered before Krishna is the name of God. The truth that was stated before Jesus existed is the name of God. Truth alone is God. God alone is the truth. That name of God which was remembered and worshipped by Dasharatha's son, Rama (in the epic, Ramayana), is the name of God. Similarly, the name of God that Devaki's son Krishna worshipped is the name of God.

Who created God?

Can God die? If God cannot die, then how can he be born?

Only he dies who is born. God exists beyond duality of life and death.

Where from did God come?

If we ponder even a little bit on the meaning of this question, we will notice an underlying belief – 'God was somewhere else, but not here. Now that he is here, he will not be present where he came from.' Does this imply that he keeps roaming from place to place? In truth God is everywhere or nowhere. The question 'where' has got to do with the concept of space; and God exists beyond concepts. The question, 'Where did he come from?' in itself is flawed. It is just like asking whether red color is straight or crooked. You will say, 'What has the color red got to do with being straight or crooked? This question itself is wrong.' Hence it is worthless to ponder over this question.

Where is God?

There can be three answers to this:

God is only within us.

God is everywhere in the world outside us.

God is both, inside and outside.

We may consider the first or the third answer to be right. In truth, God is beyond the concepts of inside and outside. The terms inside and outside exist in the language of the mind. God is beyond the reach of mind and hence God is beyond inside and outside. If God is both inside and outside, then where will it be easier to find him? It is easier to find God within us because our body is with us throughout the day. We can take a dip within whenever we like. At the same time, we also exist within God, just as a fish exists in water.

When did God create the world?

This question has to do with timing. However, the concept of time came after the world was created. It is not possible to measure something that comes first using a scale that comes later. Life exceeds and transcends time. Hence, life cannot be measured using the scale of time.

Does God have a form or is he formless?

Does God have a form and sometimes becomes formless? Or Is God formless and assumes a form? What would a common man give more importance to – gold or gold-ornaments? It will be ornaments. However, there is only one thing common to all ornaments – gold. When gold is given a form, its value appreciates in the material world. However, for the goldsmith, both gold and gold-ornaments are one and the same. A goldsmith sees gold in every gold ornament. Similarly, people give more importance to form. To the wise one, both form and formless are one and the same.

Those who believe in form and those who believe in the formless are both watching the same movie. Some are watching the part of the movie before the interval (gold), while some are watching the part after the interval (ornaments). After watching the movie, they argue on who is right. However, both of them have seen the same movie (whether it is gold or ornaments). Whether form or formless, they have known God alone.

Is God masculine? Are pictures and idols of God imaginary?

God is beyond gender and imagination. When a student is asked to describe the sky, he answers that it is yellow, if he has seen the sky at dusk. One who has seen the night sky at night would say that it is black. Someone who has seen the morning sky would say that it is blue. Similarly, a picture is formed in our minds as soon as someone mentions God. Those who have been reared according to Hindu tradition imagine a masculine God wearing a crown and ornaments on his body. This also applies to various religious beliefs around the world. Such imaginations become an obstacle in the quest for God because people remain entangled in such imagination.

If someone were to ask you to describe a doughnut, a round shape would appear in your mind. You would never imagine a square doughnut. If a square doughnut were to be made, would its taste change? However, our imagination is firm that a doughnut has to be round. God has to be masculine. If any of his embodiments have been depicted in a movie or the television by an actor, then we visualize the actor for God. Many such images of God appear on calendars and posters too. A quest based on such imagination can never attain fulfillment.

When children in kindergarten are taught words, they are shown the associated pictures. The child learns words by associating them with pictures. Later, the child can understand words without the need for the associated pictures. Similarly, pictures of God are useful initially. By progressing further on the quest, one can experience God without pictures. Those who advance from kindergarten realize that God is beyond form. Knowing God's being within us is the quest of God in the true sense.

Can the mind know God?

God is the experience beyond the mind. The mind can never know God. Only when the mind becomes still does the experience of God reveal. The mind can never accept that there can be an experience that it cannot know. People feel embarrassed to admit that they do not know and give absurd or readymade answers to avoid embarrassment.

For example, one readymade answer that is popular is that destiny results due to deeds from past births. If this birth were the result of deeds from past lives, then what was the cause of the first birth? Due to which deeds would the first birth have taken place? Man is afraid to admit that he does not know and is lost in speculative answers. It is due to such answers that imaginary concepts of God have emerged. The mind can imagine about God, but cannot experience God.

If God exists, then why is the earth full of misery?

If people are unhappy, then the remedy for their sorrow also exists and so also do doctors who have know the cure. Our job is to contact the right doctor. It is foolish to complain all the time questioning illness and sulking over why there is no cure, while refusing to visit the right doctor.

> *A priest and a barber were friends. The barber always complained about God describing the problems of the world. He always questioned, 'If God exists, then why misery is t on earth? One day, when both of them were strolling, the priest pointed at a beggar on the street and asked the barber, 'Why is that beggar's hair and beard overgrown and unkempt even when a barber like you exists?' The barber reacted, 'That's not my fault. That beggar never approached me for a haircut.' The priest explained, 'Misery exists on earth not because God does not want to eliminate it. It exists because people do not approach or connect with God. When we connect with God, all earthly miseries will vanish.'*

Why did God create both, positive and negative?

People always wonder why God has created both good and bad. For example, if you are writing a novel and you are told, 'Only create good characters in the novel', you would say, 'There cannot be an interesting story without any negative characters. This is the first requirement to write making a novel.' Similarly in life, it is essential to have both, joy and sorrow. It is essential to have both divine and demonic expressions. Without one, the other is incomplete.

Almost always, we tend to look at any incident from one angle and draw our inferences. We never pay attention to other perspectives. If God has made some people rich and some others poor, then there definitely must be a reason for it. Once you understand this, you will say, 'Yes, this is exactly how it should be.'

Today, dishonesty has risen to such a level that there is immense value for honesty. Today truth is being given importance only because untruth has become so prominent. Till the time we do not understand this and appreciate other perspectives as well, we will continue to say, 'Everything is going wrong.'

> *A king once surveyed the economic status of his kingdom. In the findings, it came to light that birds in the kingdom consumed some portion of the crop. The king began to contemplate on how the crops could be saved. He passed an order saying, 'Let all the birds be killed. People will be rewarded according to the number of birds they kill.' People began to kill the birds and soon there were none left in the kingdom. The king felt relieved thinking that the problem was now solved. But upon the next survey, the result showed a greater reduction in the stock of grains. This startled the king. On further investigation, it was found that insects and worms were eating up the grains. The king had never realized that the birds also ate a lot of insects and worms, due to which a lot of grains were actually saved. Now that there were no birds, insects and worms destroyed vast fields. Nobody had thought about this aspect.*

The intellect of man is limited. With this limited intellect, he speculates and infers that certain things are going well and certain things are going wrong. How can the limited intellect comprehend the unlimited reality? How can man's intellect grasp that huge expanse?

Man, with his little intellect, tries to bring about some improvement in what God has created. He hopes to set right whatever he believes is going wrong. When he attains wisdom, he realizes that, 'Nobody can run the activities of the world as wonderfully as they have always been running.'

If God has created both positive and negative, then why is it essential to be positive, why shouldn't we be negative?

The primary purpose of human birth is to know oneself, one's true essential nature and express the qualities of who we essentially are. For this, we need to bring the positive to the fore, bring love to the fore; we need to bring silence (which exists beyond both noise and quietness) to the fore. We need to bring happiness to the fore. The negative has been created to bring the positive to the fore. We cannot appreciate love without having known hatred.

If there is a transparent glass wall and it has nothing written on it, then anyone can walk into it. Hence it is written on the glass, "There is glass here," which warns people that a glass wall is present. Similarly, hatred, sorrow, anger, disappointment and noise have been created so that one can understand love, happiness, peace, hope, silence and compassion through these.

If God has created insane, handicapped, and poor people, then who is supposed to take care of them?

A man, who was walking along the street, came across a helpless beggar shivering with cold on the footpath. He was deeply pained at this sight and immediately gave away his overcoat. In his disappointment, he complained to God, 'After creating poverty and illness, why haven't you helped these poor people who are suffering?' The voice of God echoed in his mind, 'I have already done something for them. I have created you.'

If God has created diseases, then he has also created doctors to cure them. If he has created old, helpless, handicapped people, then he has also awakened the feeling of compassion in the minds of those who have created orphanages and shelters for such people.

Why has God created so many human bodies?

Can you tell an artist, 'Make just one picture; not many?'An artist would make all kinds of pictures to express himself. He will never be satisfied with just one. God is the artist of all artists. How can his expression be complete by creating just a few human bodies?

Why did God create this world?
What is the purpose of all this?

God is creating the world as an expression of his happiness. God and happiness are one and the same. Happiness is God's nature. Just as it is the nature of water to be wet, to flow, to be transparent and to provide coolness, God's nature is happiness, silence, creation, love. God has created the world due to his nature. Nobody asks the painter why he has made paintings. If a painter does not make a picture, he wouldn't know himself to be a painter. Similarly, God has created this phenomenal world to know himself.

What is the difference between attainment of God and God's grace?

Many consider the attainment of God to be God's grace. Attaining success or receiving help is God's grace. However, considering this to be the attainment of God, such people stop where they are, due to which their further journey does not commence. There are some who harbor the belief that, 'All my work gets done. God comes and helps me in some way or the other. Hence I have attained God.' This is a great misconception.

Being born human, to be alive, to be able to breathe is grace. But people do not recognize this. If we ask the one who is at the door of death and fighting for breath whether breathing is grace, he can only agree. Those who are healthy do not even consider being alive as grace. The definition of grace is different for them. To them grace is to attain success and a lot of wealth. If you ask the wealthy if they have attained God, their answer would be different.

God's grace has been bestowed on each of us from the very beginning. On birth, when the child comes into the world, everyone waits with baited breath for the child to take its first breath. The crying of the child is a grace. From these examples, we can understand that God's grace and the attainment of God are two different things.

Does God laugh as we do?

Ramakrishna Paramahansa once said to his disciples, 'God laughs twice. He first laughs when a doctor tells his patient, 'Do not worry. I will cure you.' Then, he laughs the second time when two people fight each other, claiming, 'This piece of land is mine.'

In the Final Truth discourses at Tejgyan, it is said that God laughs thrice. He laughs for the third time when someone imagines God to be of a particular form and that God might be laughing like man. If God is visualized as a human being, then man will also think that God should have some likes and dislikes. God will definitely laugh if He hears such things.

Is it necessary to fear God?

Fear of God is unnecessary. Various imaginations about God have given birth to fear. The fear of God was used to get good deeds done by the masses. What will be the value of that deed which is performed out of the fear of God! Noble deeds should be performed not out of the fear of God, but out of understanding, love, faith, and respect for God.

The meaning of God itself is love and love can never be angry. However, man considers God to be like him. If God becomes angry, then what is the difference between God and man? Yes, God must be definitely saddened by the fact that man thinks that he gets upset.

What is the essential mistake that man makes?

Ascribing a form to God is an essential mistake. God's taking a form is essential. The world is that form which is the need of the formless. The world is that mirror which is the face of the formless.

God is the formless, beyond the mind and the intellect. Man makes use of the mind and the intellect to understand everything. In order to teach a child it is essential to show a picture. No picture can be made of God. But understanding the need, the mistake of making pictures was made by great masters. This mistake ends on attaining God. God needs form to know himself, just as the eye needs a mirror to look at itself.

If we still have notions about God, we need to contemplate on these using common sense.

What is the idol of God? What is the idol made by God?

Man worships and respects the idol of God that he has made. But ironically, he insults and abuses the idol made by God. The idol made by God is the human body-mind. All people around us are excellent sculptures, models of imagination and idols of God Himself. Do we live with each other with a feeling of fraternity? The body is only an idol. The living energy that drives this idol is God.

It is a matter of great regret that human beings created by God, are being murdered in the name of temples and mosques. Today, nobody loves or respects the idols made by God. Hence the time has now come to bring about an awakening within ourselves and ponder to see whether we too are repeating the same mistakes that have been made by people in the past. Give your perspective a new dimension. See again in a new light with common sense.

Is it possible to converse with God?

Yes, conversation with God is possible but not in the way we think. Do not converse with God in the manner we generally do with people around us. To know something through intuition is conversation with God. God speaks with us through our own inner voice, our feelings, and intuition.

Part-III

The Three-Fold Path

CHAPTER 12

*You only perform karma. If you want to desire the fruit,
Then desire the Supreme Fruit from the Source,
not the channels.*

The Path of Karma

Actions that liberate

The concept of karma is the most entangling and grossly misunderstood concept in spirituality. We need to understand the essential meaning of 'karma'. It is not a word that can easily be explained in words from the dictionary. Most dictionary meanings till date have indicated karma to be a *result* of certain actions taking the form of our fate or destiny. This is only a partial view of the term which does not hold in all contexts. It is this partial definition that has created a puzzle out of the most profound teachings on the subject.

THE MEANING OF KARMA

From dawn to dusk, all physical and mental actions that happen through man and affect him or his surroundings are called karma. Karma is not just external visible actions. This implies that even feelings, thoughts, and spoken words are also karma because all these affect him or his surroundings. This also means that reading this book is also karma, the fruit of which you shall definitely receive.

Karma is based on the following principle: Deeds performed through the mind or body, inspired by a specific purpose, inspiration or vice, for self gain or the gain of others, have been called karma. Deeds performed with specific purpose influenced by malice, hatred, anger, fear, attachment, ego, are also karma. It is important to be aware of whether karma is taking place through the influence of vice, or from a spontaneous feeling of welfare, or from wisdom.

There is a deep correlation between karma and the fruit. Karma is the cause and the fruit is its result. In a puppet show, the dancing of the puppet is the fruit. But the karma is being performed behind the scenes; the cause for this fruit is unseen. Likewise, when a bulb glows, we can see its light, but electricity which is its cause cannot be seen. Behind every fruit, there is karma (cause). There can be no fruit without karma.

Karma is the seed; every seed yields fruit

Karma is the seed. The seeds that you sow now will later yield trees and fruits. Karma and its fruit are two sides of the same coin. We need to be vigilant about what seeds we are sowing in our life?

The seeds that you sow in the form of karma that you perform need not necessarily show their effect immediately. However, no thought, word, or deed goes in vain. The fruit is bound to come. The words uttered by us, imaginations and pictures emerging from our mind, fructify and manifest. They do not go in vain. The effect of every response manifests at some point in time.

Every karma yields its fruit. The fruit sets out towards you immediately, but it is unseen. As man is unaware of the time lag between the action and its fruit reaching him, he stops performing karma. But one who knows the principle does not stop performing karma and is saved from the adverse fruit of not performing karma.

Law of multiplicity in nature

You can easily see how many seeds exist within a fruit. However, you cannot determine how many fruits exist within a seed! The seeds that you sow fructify and yield fruit which is multiplied many times over. This is because nature returns every seed multiplied a thousand times over, be it your goodness or badness. This is the law of nature. Nature gives everything in abundance.

The vicious cycle of karma and bondage

When man knows what karma needs to be performed in any given situation and acts accordingly, then his karma does not become a cause for bondage. Fresh responses alone emerge from him in every situation. Man performs deeds according to preconditioning or prior programming. In every incident, he gives out the same old reaction in unconsciousness. This is bondage. By observing the habits and tendencies of a person in bondage, it can be easily predicted as to how he would react in a given situation. If someone abuses him, he may instantly erupt with anger. If he receives praise, he may be immediately pleased. Thus, man in bondage works just like a machine where there is no thinking or understanding that backs his karma.

First, karma yields fruit and then that fruit induces further karma, which begets further fruit. In this manner man remains entangled in this vicious cycle of karma and bondage. People fail to understand how they can come out of this vicious cycle of karma and bondage; they continue to be entangled in the fruit of karma.

***Karmatma* - The soul of karma**

Karmatma (the soul of karma) is born through the union of Love, Right Intention and Understanding. When there is love and reverence in karma, it becomes impersonal. If this understanding is missing, then the soul of karma is weak. When love, intention and understanding are all present, then the soul of karma is very strong.

Without higher understanding, the soul of karma dies. Without the soul of karma, actions that arise are dead karma. Such dead actions that are devoid of the soul of karma only bring despair. Actions performed with a strong *Karmatma* open the doors to enlightenment.

When actions are surrendered unto God, then such

actions are devoid of the desire for fruit. When the feeling of doership is absent, then actions do not bind. Therefore, it is important to know what kind of feelings and intentions should be there behind any action.

The significance of feelings and intentions

If karma is not performed with the right intention, it becomes the cause of bondage. If you desire that your actions should not bind you, then you ought to be alert while performing karma. When you're performing karma, you can ask yourself, 'Why am I performing this action? What is my true intention or feeling behind it?' You need to honestly enquire before performing the deed; you would then be alert. After you become alert, you will be able to understand that the fruit that ensues depends on the feeling or intention behind your deeds.

Let us understand this with an example. At the end of a session in a court of law, when the judge announces his verdict that the accused is sentenced to death, what is the kind of karma that the judge is performing? Would this karma result in bondage? For those who believe in rebirth and the extension of karma across lifetimes, will the prisoner become a judge in his next life and sentence this judge? What would be the fruit that the executioner incurs for the deed of hanging the accused? The executioner's only job is to hang people to death. Will this seemingly gruesome act of the executioner bind him? The judge and the executioner will not attract any untoward results. If there is no feeling of doership in the deed performed, then bondage will not result. At the time of announcing the sentence, if the judge nurtures a feeling of vengeance or contempt, then the deed would bear an undesirable fruit.

The original sin

You ought to first recognize and rectify the original sin. Living the life of a separate individual (the true ego, characterized by the sense of apparent separateness from the rest of creation) is the original sin.

Man always contemplates on the second sin (the false ego, characterized by exaggerated self-pride); he never pays attention to the first sin. If he first attends to the original sin, the second sin will not occur. The first sin is only one, while the second sin is in multiples. If you want to be saved from the many subsequent sins, then attend to the first original sin. Man forgets his true identity and lives the life of a separate limited individual in ignorance. Actions that arise based on the assumed individual identity are sin; actions that arise based on the understanding of the true identity are the greatest virtue.

Your deeds have a lasting effect on the universe. When more and more people awaken to the truth by realizing their true identity, then their deeds will raise the level of consciousness of the entire universe. The actions that arise from people in ignorance tend to lower the level of consciousness. As the level of consciousness drops, the obstacles and troubles of the world rise. One who is able to see this clearly becomes aware of his responsibility to eliminate the troubles of the world.

The trap of reactive living

If a person curses or abuses you and you too retort in the same way, you are being reactive. Had the person not abused you, you too would not have abused him. This shows that your act of abusing or not abusing him is dependent on the action of the other person. This is the reactive way of living.

When the understanding of the science of karma is internalized by you, then you would continue to give the other person due respect, even if he does not praise you or abuses you. Your respecting him is not dependent on his action. If your actions are dependent upon others, then such actions are reactions. It is only understanding of the truth that can transform you from a reactive way of living into creative life where all your actions are backed by love, higher intention, and wisdom.

THREE REASONS FOR BONDAGE TO KARMA

1. Doership

Most often, actions are performed with a feeling of doership wherein one arrogates credit by feeling 'I did it'. While working or after performing karma, people feel, 'I made this happenÖ How great I amÖ Nothing can happen without meÖ' or 'Oh! I shouldn't have done thisÖ it's wrongÖ' With such feelings, the individual 'I' (the ego) is strengthened. It is this thought of personal 'I' that becomes the reason for bondage to karma.

Some people who are aware that the ego is the cause of bondage to karma try to circumvent this by avoiding the use of the word 'I'. They feel that by not using the word 'I', they would not be bound to karma. This is a gross misconception. Even without using the word 'I', if they harbor the feeling of 'I did it', their sense of doership is still strong. The fruits are commensurate with whatever feeling one harbors while acting.

> *The root thought of 'I' needs to be uprooted with the fire of higher understanding. When man attains higher understanding, then none of the karma performed through his body will bind him. After obtaining higher understanding, man experiences true happiness of liberation for the first time. With the knowledge of the science of karma, you can know the root cause of bondage to actions and also obtain liberation from it. When there is no doership, then there is no possibility of being bound to the fruit of action.*

2. Tendencies and habits

You would have seen waterfalls in the mountains. When water flows along the mountainous terrain, it carves pathways. Once such pathways are made, the water follows the same course every time. When the rainy season ends, the water dries up; but it is highly possible that water flows along the same course, the same pathways, in the next rainy season. This is repeated year after year and the pathways become more entrenched with every season. There is no need for the water to put in any extra effort to find new pathways. The effort was required only for the first time, as the water had to create the first pathway by moving obstacles such as rocks and vegetation. Subsequently, following the beaten path becomes very easy.

This is exactly what happens with man. By repeating the same behavior or thought again and again, a pattern or tendency is formed. The pathway that is created is called habit. He continues to react as per the same patterns. As he repeats his preconditioned behavior, his tendencies become deep-rooted.

The habit of doing any deed in the same way again and again is tendency. Man is not alert before or while acting. He never thinks, 'Why am I doing this work, how am I doing it?' From morning till night, all the deeds that happen through you are the unconscious enactment of tendencies. This predisposition of flowing as per one's tendencies becomes the cause for bondage to karma.

Two pages are stacked together in front of you and you are given a pen. When you write something on the first page, the impressions of what is being written also get imprinted on the second page. This can be seen on closer inspection of the second page. This implies that although work was being performed on the first page, subtle impressions were created on the second page. If you run a brush that is dipped in carbon powder on the second page, the subtle lines become clearer. These lines are food for the contrast mind. The contrast mind runs in these lines of subtle impressions. Just as the pig finds contentment in dwelling in gutters, the contrast mind abides in these impressions that are created by actions.

Not everyone creates impressions with the same intensity on the next page. One who is under the influence of anger, fear or greed applies more pressure while writing. Applying more pressure implies that he gets attached and identifies himself with the pen and paper. He has thus become the pen, as it were. He further identifies with the paper on which he is writing. Due to this attachment, the pen and paper are no longer distinct. The pen does not even rise above the paper while writing, thereby creating deeper impressions and repeating the same impressions again and again.

In the above analogy, the pen is the body that has been attained on birth. The page is the field of activity where man performs actions. In the beginning, when man begins to write (act), impressions are very subtle. But later, these impressions became deeper and more engrained. Now due to these impressions (habits), a tendency is formed and due to these tendencies, man mechanically manifests anger, fear or greed. Even though he does not desire to be angry, it has now become a habit. Once a tendency is formed, he is easily drawn to act according to the tendency. If man becomes even a little unconscious, he then starts moving along the same lines as per his past impressions. Patterns and tendencies are created due to unconsciousness and ignorance. If patterns and tendencies are to be broken, then raising the level of consciousness is very important.

3. The air of arrogation

A child does not consider itself to be the body. The child is established in the experience of the Self and thus devoid of the false feeling of being the body. In childhood, there is no individual 'I' that takes credit for performing a task by saying 'I did it'. Subsequently, when the child grows up, he started blowing the air of 'I' to the deeds that are performed through the body. Owing to the blowing of this air into the false 'I', man started receiving false pleasure. He gets entangled in this false pleasure.

When he started receiving false happiness by considering himself to be a separate body, he gets distanced from the original bliss. He is lost to his essence due to indiscriminate indulgence in material pleasure for the rest of his life.

Expect from the Source and not from the channels

Man is unhappy both ways: when he does not get the fruit of the work he performed, and also when he does get the fruit. If he gets the fruit, he mistakes the channel from which he is getting the fruit to be the source. As a result, he expects further fruit from the same channel and becomes disheartened if the channel does not deliver the goods. If his brother who used to help him earlier, stops helping him, he says, 'My brother has let me down.' If the father does not assign a share of his property to the son, then the son starts hating his father. This is so because, people consider their relatives to be the 'givers' or the 'Source'. In the Indian scripture, the *Gita,* it is said, *'Perform action without desiring the fruit.'* This is because man is unaware of the punishment that he invites by getting stuck to the fruit. It may so happen that he may forget God, the ultimate source. When this happens, what bigger loss could befall him? If God were to state the couplet again, he would say, *'Perform action with Me and desire the fruit in plenty. Things go wrong when you desire the fruit from the channel.'* Or it can also be said, *'Sow the seed of faith and then desire in plenty, but only from the Source.'*

Let us understand this. When we need water, we draw it from the tap. Does the tap have any capacity of giving? The tap is merely a channel and not the Source. There are many taps (channels) *through* which water is received, but they all come from the same water tank in the building. We insist that we want water only from a particular tap. If you seek water directly from the tank, you will get more than you could ever ask for. It is common sense to expect from the Source, rather than the channel. Everything is in abundance in the Source. You may become tired of receiving from the Source, but the Source is never tired of giving, since everything is ever-plentiful there. When you desire from the Source (God), then you will be told *"Perform action and desire the supreme fruit from the Source and not from the channel."*

When you understand this secret, then you will begin to desire the supreme fruit of self-realization.

Bright understanding: The greatest of all karma

We need to perform the greatest karma of understanding the truth to liberate ourselves from the bondage of karma. Obtaining understanding is the greatest karma. We need to first understand the root cause of bondage. If we strike at the root of bondage of actions then all subsequent actions will arise from awareness and understanding. Such actions will not cause bondage.

There's a subtle missing link here which needs to be grasped. What is important – the actions that we perform, or the thoughts that arise in the mind after the action? With understanding, it becomes clear that actions are no doubt important, but not as much as the perspective that we carry *after* the action is complete. Actions and events would happen anyways; there is no escape from action, because even inaction is a form of action. However, the commentary that occurs in the mind after the action is performed is vital.

After the triggering thought spurs us into action appears, the action simply happens. However, the mental commentary after the action either brings a feeling of acceptance or non-acceptance. One then needs to assess whether this action ought to be surrendered to God or arrogated to oneself. When the fruit of action is mentally surrendered to God with the conviction that he alone is the real doer, it brings forth the supreme fruit of self-realization.

Let us understand what 'fruit of action' implies here. If a student clears his exam with good grades, then the result of the exam is not the fruit of action. Herein lies the missing link. There are only three kinds of fruits for any action – sorrow, happiness, and dilemma. In this example, if the student is depressed despite getting good grades because he expected a better result, then the unhappiness of the student is the fruit of action. If on the contrary, the student is happy about having barely passed the examination, then the fruit of action is happiness. Understand that we should neither look at the events nor its external result, because the actual fruit is internal – it is happiness, sorrow, or dilemma that ensues from the external result.

Whenever an event occurs, we need to look within and evaluate: *What happened at the thought level?* If there is sorrow, then surrender the sorrow to God. If there is happiness, instead of assuming 'I became happy', know that 'This happiness too is God's' and surrender it unto him. If you surrender only sorrows and arrogate happiness to yourself, then that too would result in sorrow alone. If there is dilemma, then the dilemma must also be offered to God.

In this way, every fruit, if offered to God, brings forth the supreme fruit. There would then be no attachment and the fruit will not become the cause of bondage.

Perform Bright Action by being the Self-witness

We need to shift our focus from external actions to the feelings or intentions that back them. The feeling of being a witness needs to be brought into every action. The constant awareness should be that actions are happening *through* this body, not by me. I am not the doer.

After becoming a witness to every action, we need to go even further. Most people stop after attaining the witness perspective. They remain aware that the body is going around, action is happening, etc. But the story of karma does not end here. In order to perform the highest actions that liberate, we need to shift from being a witness to being the Self-witness.

While watching all the activities as a mere witness, one needs to shift to the awareness of the Self. When every activity, every event leads you to your essential presence, to the awareness of the Self, you stay in the seat of your 'Being' and perform all acts. At this stage, you are only present. All actions happen in your presence. Actions performed in such a state are not reactions. All work performed in this way is Bright action. Such actions do not bind. Such deeds have the power to destroy the effects of countless past deeds. With the right understanding, the fire of knowledge can destroy all past karma. Otherwise, it would appear impossible to attain liberation from past karma.

Action that is not backed by knowledge is useless. Many a time, such action can become life threatening. Hence, such actions should be destroyed with the fire of knowledge. A mouse keeps gnawing away at a basket the whole night and makes a hole. Anyone who watches this would think that the mouse is working hard all night. But in the morning, a snake appears from within the basket through the hole and devours the mouse. Had someone warned the mouse of the consequences of making a hole in the basket, the mouse would have been grateful to him for the knowledge. In the same way, if we understand the consequences of actions on time, then we too can improve the actions being performed in the present.

After attaining the final understanding, man realizes the One who is actually performing actions through various bodies. After attaining this understanding, actions are performed towards attaining the whole and sole objective of life – stabilizing in the experience of the Self followed by self-expression.

Bright Action *(Tej Karma)*

When a man uses a chisel and hammer to carve a line on stone, this line remains for a long period. Likewise, some deeds are such that they are remembered by man throughout his life. He suffers the pain of remorse for such deeds all through his life. If he nurtures hatred towards anyone, he burns in this feeling of hatred every moment of his life. Deeds that affect man throughout his life are like lines carved on stone.

Some deeds are like lines drawn on sand. The effects of such deeds last only for some time. After a brief period, the effects of such deeds vanish.

There are some deeds that are akin to lines drawn on

water. When lines are drawn in water, they vanish as soon as they are made. Such deeds bear fruit immediately.

Finally, there are some deeds that are like lines drawn in the sky. You know that lines cannot be drawn in the sky. Bright deeds are like the lines drawn in the sky. Such deeds do not result in bondage. The bondage of such deeds is exhausted even before it is created! Hence, we should keep the objective of being in the state where Bright deeds happen through us.

Bright fresh actions originate from the One who has attained self-realization. The impressions of prior tendencies no longer exist. He always remains in the present and all his responses arise from the knowledge of his true identity. Even if a neighbor who has earlier had a tussle with him approaches him, he gives his neighbor a bright, fresh response. The thought never occurs that his neighbor had behaved badly with him. Recognizing his true identity as well as the true identity of the neighbor, Bright actions arise from him.

When man merges in God, then Bright actions emerge. This is because God is the doer of all actions. The world springs into life every morning by the mere presence of the sun. Activities get performed owing to the presence of the sun. However, the sun is not the doer; deeds happen in its presence. In the same way, the body is merely available to the divine presence and serves as the medium for self-expression. Just as a spinning top appears stationary whilst spinning at top speed, similarly though countless actions happen in his presence, he still appears actionless!

CHAPTER 13

The death of the student leads to the birth of the seeker;
The death of the seeker leads to the birth of the disciple;
The death of the disciple leads to the birth of the devotee;
Upon the death of the devotee emerges the One who is unborn.... the Self.

The path of devotion

The catalyst that speeds the quest

It is not mandatory that a devotee should build holy places of worship to express his love for God. Our body is indeed a temple of God. With true devotion, the devotee resolves to make his body a temple. With the practice of devotion, he throws all impurities and vices out of his body-mind. His body then begins to radiate with the brilliance of pure love. Do we have such Bright love for God? Can we build at least one temple for God? Our very own body-mind is this temple, which should be rid of the filth of beliefs, patterns and tendencies.

WHAT IS DEVOTION ?

Devotion is the love for Love itself. To understand this in its essence, one ought to understand the phrase 'God is Love; Love is God.' Why is it said that God is Love? Let us understand this with an example.

What would you say about a person who takes countless photographs of himself in different forms, in different costumes, at various places? You would say that he is in love with himself. In the same way, God, through His power to manifest himself, assumes innumerable forms. All the living beings of this world are his creation, his photographs. Can you imagine how much God loves himself!? He endlessly goes on discarding old pictures every day and creates new ones. He is ever engaged in creating pristine and innovative colorful pictures. Hence, it is said that God is Love. When you truly start loving God, it implies that there is love for Love itself. Devotion is the love for Love.

Devotion can be practiced anywhere. One need not necessarily visit holy places of worship to think about and feel God. On the contrary, one may visit holy places and not think about God at all. Understand that every place is his. Therefore, devotion can be practiced anywhere, anytime, whenever one gets the opportunity.

Should the body or the mind have devotion? Our body bows down in places of worship, but has our mind ever bowed down? The mind, which is the hurdle in the attainment of the supreme quest, needs to bow down. It can then express devotion through the medium of the body.

Devotion is not a path, but the goal in itself. This is one of the major missing links in spirituality. Devotion by itself is a great fruit; devotion in itself is bliss. The common belief is that God will be pleased if we have devotion. The truth is that devotion takes place *when God is pleased.*

The Devotee is a Drop in the Ocean of God

The ocean is the primeval source of water. The ocean is also the centre, the confluence where water from all the waterfalls, rivers, canals, and mountains come and mingle together. The ocean is symbolic of God and the individual flows of water represent man. This is just an example to understand the relationship between a devotee and God.

The surface water of the ocean evaporates and rises towards the skies and forms clouds. Some of the clouds may travel far and wide to various lands. These clouds then precipitate and take the form of rain. When clouds above the ocean produce rain, the rain water falls back to merge into the ocean. Man is like a drop of rain that assumes a temporary existence of his own, separate from the ocean. Just like the rain drop, man too journeys through time to reunite with God, attaining the original nature of unlimited bliss.

But does all rain water fall directly into the ocean? No. Some water which rains on distant lands, in mountainous terrain gets stuck in ditches or reservoirs. The water then begins to stagnate. Similarly, people forget their basic purpose of existence and get stuck in their lives in worthless pursuits. Just as water from the various ditches and puddles get swept into rivers, to join the course towards the ocean, similarly, when man recollects his true aim, he gets the right direction. Devotion is like the river that leads one to the ocean of God.

When rain water flows towards the ocean, it imagines about the ocean. But it does not know that the ocean is beyond its imagination. The ocean has no banks and its depth cannot be fathomed. Similarly, a seeker also imagines God, his form, his potential. He does not know that God is beyond the grasp of the limited intellect.

When the drop falls into the river, it simply surrenders itself to the flow of the river and finally merges into the ocean. Similarly, when man is graced with devotion, his mind surrenders completely, without any objection and journeys ahead till he loses his individual identity in the grandeur of the Self.

Potential of Devotion

Several blessings have already been bestowed on man, but man is just unaware of the grace that is being showered on him continuously. One needs to enhance one's eligibility to attain the grace of devotion. This grace transforms the thirst for truth into divine love. It is this divine love alone that liberates us from worldly illusions and reunites us with God.

Devotion alone paves the way for attainment of the experience of God. Words fall short of expressing this most beautiful experience, which can only be felt through feelings of total acceptance and surrender. The devotee who has experienced the Self, who lives in the bliss of God-realization, incessantly expresses his devotion in various ways. He may shed tears, sing hymns, dance in ecstasy, express the divine experience in words, or remain in silence. Such devotees bring about a great revolution and help in raising the level of mass consciousness.

When you have the conviction that devotion is the most beautiful gift, then alone will devotion blossom within you. You then begin to witness miracles in your life. Till such time that devotion is not awakened, it does not feel good. But once devotion is awakened then everything else becomes insignificant.

You need not leave the illusory world in order to attain the heights of supreme devotion. Just as the lotus blooms in dirty water and yet retains its resplendence, you too can be engaged in the marketplace, performing all your duties and responsibilities perfectly, without being lost in the web of delusion. Just as water does not remain on the lotus leaf due to its waxy surface, the vices of the world such as hatred or ego cannot survive in the presence of devotion.

Ego is the problem; devotion is the solution

In order to attain happiness, man gets entangled in various pursuits of the world. However, worldly pursuits only provide temporary joy. True happiness does not lie in the external world. Wisdom and devotion alone can help in attaining permanent bliss.

When man derives long term happiness in worldly objects, there cannot be a greater loss. He would never go in the quest of the truth. As a result, he will not be able to experience the bliss of devotion, which he is heir to. The thirst for truth arouses devotion in man.

Man's root desire is to realize and express the Self (God). Whenever man is seeking the truth, he is actually engaged in devotion. When he realizes that his actual desire behind all the superficial needs is to realize the truth, he then starts remaining in the state of true devotion. He starts praying for fulfillment of this ultimate purpose.

When man begins to remain in devotion with understanding, his ego begins to fall. True devotion is a state in which the devotee disappears. True service is that in which the one who serves, dissolves. True wisdom is that in which the one who has wisdom surrenders. True meditation is that in which the one who meditates is lost.

ASCEND THE TEN GRADES OF DEVOTION

When you study in school, you pass through various grades (classes) till you graduate. Similarly, there are ten grades of devotion that man ascends in the quest for truth. The disposition of the devotee decides what grade he is in. Let us understand how devotion matures as one ascends these grades.

Grade I: Blind devotion

At grade I, devotion is blind, as it does not have the eyes of wisdom or understanding. The devotee blindly follows ritual mongers who ask him to become an ascetic, wear saffron robes, confuse him with rituals, rosaries, offerings, giving of alms, etc. He gets entangled in various beliefs and rituals. He dwells in the imagination of the joys of heaven. For him, devotion is a form of entertainment, which is shallow and short-lived. Such a person is not truly a devotee as he may appear from his external facade. Internally, he has his personal selfish agenda. He shows as if he is ardent; however, he could be merely showing off.

When devotion arises out of blind faith in ignorance and unconsciousness, it shakes in the face of calamities. The devotee is not stable and his faith keeps shaking due to lack of understanding. He is ignorant of the truth. Such a devotee has to come out of this ignorance to progress on his journey. He has to listen to the truth and contemplate on it.

As the understanding of the seeker increases, he ascends to the second grade of devotion.

Grade II: Karmic devotion

When the seeker progresses into second grade, he gains the understanding that everything is a game of karma. His devotion hinges around the cycle of his actions and their results. The seeker begins to understand that he will reap fruit according to the actions that he performs. If he performs good actions, he gets good results; if his actions are bad, he attracts bad results. Hence, he performs virtuous deeds and refrains from evil.

At this stage, devotion takes the shape of repentance for bad deeds performed in the past. He feels a sense of adulation for God thinking that God has showered so much grace on him, despite all the sins that he has committed in the past. The devotee assumes that he has to repent or 'make up' for the sinful actions of his past. With this intention, his level of consciousness is raised to a certain extent.

At this level, the devotee is not able to think on answers to more fundamental questions such as, 'If his current birth is because of his past actions, then due to which actions was his first birth.' When he is successful in his endeavors, he admires his own actions; if he fails, he curses his destiny. His actions are devoid of true devotion, due to which his ego keeps bloating.

Grade III: Devotion of multiple gods

Upon entering the third grade, questions arise within the seeker's mind as to who provides us with the various fruits of our actions. Who is it, who decides as to what fruit should be given for which action? Who decides the time of fructification of the action? As these questions gain depth, his desire for the answers intensifies.

After contemplating and taking others' opinions, he begins to believe in God in various forms or deities. He starts selectively worshipping the various deities to address his personal needs. This is more relevant in the Indian context. The devotion takes the form of business transactions. In return for his devotion, the devotee expects God to fulfill his desires. The devotion is thus conditional. He believes that God exists as the various idols that represent various deities. Forms were conceived only to convey the Formless. However, he misses this point and engages in idol worship. If he does not get what he desires after worshipping one deity, he shifts to another, believing that there are multiple gods.

Grade IV: Singular devotion

Man has imagined God in various forms. Assuming God to be manifold, he prays to different Gods, but when man does not get the fruit of his prayer, his faith in God reduces.

After being subject to such disillusionment, the devotee enters the fourth grade of devotion wherein his understanding matures further. He comes to realize that God is not manifold, but One. All prayers ultimately reach only one source. After getting into the fourth grade, the devotee prays, knowing God to be the one source of everything. He thus prepares to shift his focus from the various forms to the formless, absolute, unlimited God. His fear of God is replaced by reverence. This is called singular devotion.

Grade V: Devotion for the guru

In the fifth grade of devotion, the seeker's desire to attain the supreme truth is awakened and he comes to know that proper guidance is essential to attain the truth. Only a living guru can impart the right guidance; hence the seeker sets out in search of the guru. On receiving the guru and attaining understanding from the guru, the seeker realizes that the final truth can be attained only from the guru. He begins to know that the guru is not just a body; He is indeed the Self. The guru's external body merely serves as an instrument for the guru or Self to awaken within. When this understanding deepens, it gives rise to a deep feeling of love and reverence for the guru.

The devotee's love for the guru's instructions liberates him from all kinds of sorrows and vices. It is only in the feeling of love and reverence for the guru that the seeker abides by all his instructions. The instructions of the guru are meant to make the seeker's mind pure, unshaken, and loving. When the seeker abides by the guru's instructions, his life begins to be filled with amazement, bliss, and devotion. He gets liberated from every so-called problem by the guru's grace. Devotion for the guru leads to the dissolution of the ego that separates the seeker from the guru.

Grade VI: Divine devotion

To begin with, the devotee prays to God to achieve his selfish ends. One may desire a good job, success, cure from illness, one may long for an offspring, freedom from worries, etc. This is known as materialistic devotion. The devotee needs to surmount the trench of materialistic devotion and reach the heights of divine devotion. After the disciple receives understanding from the guru in the fifth grade, he attains divine devotion in the sixth grade.

With Divine devotion, the devotee is liberated from all desires except the single auspicious desire, which is expressed in the feeling: 'O God! Enough of this endless pursuit of the world! None of the worldly pleasures can now satisfy me. Now, I will be satisfied only after attaining you.' With this feeling, he prays to God from the bottom of his heart.

The mother tries to engross her child with newer toys. In the attraction of these toys, the child forgets his mother. But one day the child pushes aside all his toys and starts crying for his mother. The mother has to then leave all her work aside and come to the child. In the same way, in the sixth grade, the devotee gets fed up of the toys of illusion and becomes determined that he wants only God. In divine devotion, the disciple's desire for attainment of God intensifies. He then ascends to the seventh grade.

Grade VII: Divine Submission

Man makes various offerings such as fruits, flowers, wealth, service, etc. to God. When he attains the understanding that whatever he offers belongs to God from the very beginning, then his ego begins to melt with the feeling of devotion.

This understanding deepens, until one fine day he realizes that the one who is offering also belongs to God. With this understanding, the ego which was surviving based on an assumed separateness from God, surrenders. At this stage of devotion, the feeling of a separate 'I' that was formed due to ignorance of the Truth is surrendered completely. When devotion takes the form of divine submission, the mind experiences the happiness of submitting to the will of God. The mind stops taking credit for whatever is done when it understands that God alone does everything.

Grade VIII: Divine Acceptance

Till the devotee reaches the eighth grade, he has the intense auspicious desire for attaining the Truth. However, this auspicious desire is also nothing but a desire. At the eighth grade, this desire also is also surrendered. The devotee is able to accept easily that even if the truth is not attained, he will remain devoted; he has no qualms about anything. Here, the devotee lives in the feeling of total acceptance. With total acceptance comes real happiness.

For the devotee who has ascended till such heights of devotion, it is indeed very painful to accept that 'it is acceptable even if the truth is not attained'. However, when this is accepted by him completely, then the attainment of truth becomes very easy. If the devotee tries to short-circuit the process by giving up the desire for the truth earlier in the journey, believing that he can then attain God, then this is not acceptance; it is ignorance. If there is the slightest trace of greed in the feeling of acceptance, then it is not acceptance at all. Hence, it is necessary that the feeling of acceptance arises from the right understanding.

Grade IX: Divine Wisdom

In the search of the final truth, the seeker, having been through all the paths of devotion, finally attains the final understanding. He understands through self experience that the devotee and God are not separate, there is only One. He realizes that it is God who was seeking Himself by becoming a devotee.

Treading the path of wisdom, the seeker initially proceeds with knowledge and his search culminates in devotion. In the same way, the devotee who begins his journey with devotion finally attains wisdom. With wisdom, the seeker becomes a true devotee and remains ever-immersed in the bliss of devotion. When the seeker attains the truth, there is a blending of wisdom and devotion. He experiences the supreme truth, which is beyond all imagination.

At this stage, all the secrets are unveiled. The devotee merges into God, just as the river merges into the ocean. This is self-realization. Here the reality of the illusory world unfolds and the universal consciousness is revealed. This experience cannot be described in words. It can only be known through experience, as it is beyond the body, mind, and intellect.

Grade X: Bright Divine devotion

Now, if the devotee and God become one, then what else remains to be done? In the tenth grade, the devotee and God once again become two from the One! This is a matter of great depth.

After becoming a devotee again, he starts getting amazed by the various things which begin to manifest in life so easily. He now has the divine eye to witness the wonders of the world. He becomes a child again. With the awakening of

Bright Divine devotion, he begins to observe these wonders, being established in the Silence. This astonishment is not invented by the mind; rather, it is the amazement that results after the dissolution of the contrast mind.

Devotion is not attachment

Before true devotion awakens, man has attachment to people and objects of the illusory world. He presumes this attachment to be love. However, there is vast difference between devotion and attachment. In attachment, man can indulge indiscriminately to any extent. The end of attachment is only grief; whereas the end of true devotion is unconditional bliss.

Whenever you want to free yourself from an attachment, then you get into another attachment. In other words, you come out of one form of illusion by using another form of illusion. This is of no use in the ultimate sense, as you are abiding in illusion, instead of the truth. You are not in devotion; you are in the state of affection or attachment for the external world. Devotion is when you are attached to the truth which is beyond the mind. For example, when you get thoughts of grief and you switch on the music system or the TV, it means you have used the radio, which is an object of the material world, to escape from grief. You then become attached to the radio that it should not stop or break down. However, if it breaks down for some reason, then this becomes a new cause of grief for you. Thus, you get into an endless chain of attachment to worldly objects, which never satisfies you. True devotion alone can bring you out of this web of delusion and establish you in unconditional and unbroken happiness.

Impediments in devotion

Devotion needs to be kept alive with contemplation. Whenever it is felt that the feeling of devotion is reducing, it means that the recognition of truth is becoming hazy. At such junctures, the recognition of truth can be raised by listening to the truth, reading literature on truth, and mainly through contemplation. We need to introspect as to what are the beliefs that exist within us due to which the recognition of the truth is becoming hazy. When such questions are asked, such beliefs come to light and are eradicated. Thus the temple, in the form of your body, gets cleansed. The light of wisdom and the fragrance of love engulf the whole temple!

Initially when a person hears about the greatness of devotion, he could become obsessive about becoming a 'great' devotee. Treading on the path of devotion, when his mind becomes pure and sacred, he begins to imagine that his is the 'best' devotion. The desire that 'mine has to be the best devotion' is the play of the ego. Devotion can never be greater or better than others, because devotion is a gift which is complete in itself. Due to ego, man feels that he should keep ahead of others in the race for devotion as well! When this desire is eradicated from the mind, then the heights of devotion begin to manifest on its own.

Devotion filled response after recognition of the truth

In devotion, we should understand as to whom we are giving response in our daily life. When response to the Self alone arises through us in situations of daily life, then Divine devotion is awakened.

When the conviction that God's desire alone is my desire arises within you, then devotion filled response arises on its own from within you. Such a response that is filled with devotion paves the way to real bliss. Although the ego does not derive anything from devotion filled response, yet the mind will feel the bliss. For example, when you cook food for someone and the person likes the food, you experience happiness. You feel the happiness even if you are fasting that day and do not have food yourself. Why do you get this happiness? You neither had the food, nor did you taste it. You will say, "I am happy because the one for whom I made the food liked it." The right response was given to the one who was receiving the food. Thus, the right response was given to the one for whom the response was meant. When the feeling, 'In God's happiness alone lies my happiness' arises within you, then the right response arises through you, which is based on recognition of the Truth.

When you practice devotion filled response out of love in daily circumstances, your devotion increases day by day. You become that which you focus on. When your life becomes a response filled with love for God, you are focusing on divinity in and through your daily activities. This paves the way to becoming Divine.

CHAPTER **14**

Every worldly task is done with the help of the mind... Meditation is the only thing that happens when there is no mind.

The path of meditation

Our essential nature

Meditation is not attention. Meditation is neither concentration nor contemplation. In India, the word 'meditation' has come from spiritual scriptures. Spiritual seekers understood the deeper aspects of meditation. However, in today's world the meaning of meditation is totally misconstrued. The words 'attention', 'contemplation' and 'meditation' have been used interchangeably. Therefore, the word meditation has lost its deeper significance.

Meditation is a quality of the Self, an attribute of your essential nature. Meditation is the source which is present regardless of whether we are in the state of deep sleep or in waking state.

The simple meaning of meditation is 'doing nothing'. However, some people find 'doing nothing' very difficult. They *try to do* 'nothing' instead of 'doing nothing'. They question as to how it is possible to do 'nothing'. It is like asking, "What should I *do* to get sleep?" You have to do *nothing* to get sleep. You just need to lie down and you will be asleep. If you try hard to get sleep, then your very attempt to sleep will prevent you from getting sleep. Otherwise, it is an effortless process. Similarly, meditation is a process in which you do not need to do anything; your very presence in essence is meditation.

Whenever we are entangled in the objects of the external world such as relationships, wealth, status, or power, all our senses get completely engrossed in them. Meditation, when viewed as a path, is a technique that liberates us from the outside world and directs us within, onto the experience of Being. All our senses, which are focused on the external world, should be redirected to return within. This is the initial preparation for entering into meditation wherein the eye returns onto the eye, i.e. the eye feels or experiences itself; the ear returns onto the ear. All the senses feel and experience themselves. When the senses return onto themselves, they are then helpful for us to go within.

It is also important to understand that liberation from the external world is not the real purpose. This is only the preparation for the real purpose – Self Meditation. Due to this missing link, meditation has been restricted to the practice of sitting in solitude with eyes shut.

SELF-MEDITATION

The meaning of the word 'meditation' has been corrupted as it has been grossly misunderstood to be 'concentration'. As a result, people focus on techniques pertaining to the body and only attain a high degree of concentration. The primary purpose behind these techniques is to stabilize in the state of Beingness followed by expression that arises from that state. In order to refer to this original purpose without causing confusion, a new term has been introduced: Self-meditation.

Self-meditation is being one with the Source or being established in the seat of 'Being'[1]. When you reach the seat of Being, it can be said that you are in Self-meditation. Only then is meditation focused on meditation itself. Other terms that can be used are Self-witness or Bright meditation.

---

1. The technique of accessing the state of Beingness that exists beyond all concepts and conditions is imparted in the MA retreat.

During meditation, all kinds of thoughts arise. These thoughts torment us only because we get attached and identified with them. You are *the witness of* these thoughts. You are not the thoughts. All the thoughts that are buried deep within you have to emerge and are encountered by the witness. The mind thus gets annihilated in this process. Knowing the Knower of all experiences in and through every experience is Self-meditation.

Many a time, on seeing pictures of sages and saints sitting in meditation with eyes shut, it is misunderstood that they are in Self-meditation. One can never judge from the external appearance as to whether a person is meditating or is in the state of Self-meditation. Many people sit with closed eyes. Externally, they may appear to be in the state of Self-meditation. It is possible that they are internally filled with various thoughts.

Nobody knows what death is and therefore people are afraid of dying. Similarly, we do not know what happens in meditation. Hence, our mind fears it. After attaining understanding of the truth, it becomes easy for the mind to enter into the depths of meditation. In Self-meditation, the Self, who is the experiencer, experiences the experiencer, in every experience.

In reality, Self-meditation is the fruit, the result after reaching the ultimate goal of stabilizing in the state of self-realization. Once self-stabilization is attained, you are always in meditation; rather, you become Self-meditation.

Benefits of Meditation

Benefits of meditation can be broadly classified under the following categories.

1. Physical Level

- Higher efficiency.
- The moment your identification with the body breaks, physical sufferings cease to exist.
- With non-identification with your body, you can even be liberated from death.

2. Mental Level

- The ability to concentrate increases, thereby increasing memory retention and retrieval. In the process, the unsteadiness of the mind decreases.
- Freedom from stress.
- Awareness increases, you become more peaceful and stable.
- Meditation brings a change in your thoughts. The chaos that exists in thoughts reduces to a great extent. Thoughts are well directed. Simplicity seeps in. Thinking ability increases. Many things about the mind become clear to you, which otherwise you would have never known.
- With meditation, if the understanding of 'Who am I?' grows, then it leads to freedom from all misconceptions, resulting in the end of all misery.

3. Financial Level

- With improved efficiency you improve in your profession or business, thereby generating and managing wealth more effectively.

4. Social Level

- With meditation, you are filled with boundless happiness leading to harmony with one and all.

5. Spiritual Level

- Meditation helps in realising your true nature or realising the answer to the question – 'Who am I?'
- With meditation you reach the state of *Samadhi*[2]. You develop conviction in the state of *Samadhi*. If reverence for the truth arises within you, then it becomes easier to go within onto oneself. You realise that meditation is your essential nature which is present since the very beginning.

---

2. Samadhi refers to the timeless state of being that exists before the world was created

- Once self-realisation is attained, seeing you, others too are inspired to attain that ultimate bliss. Due to this desire, they too become truth seekers and ultimately attain the final knowledge.

Mistakes committed in the practice of meditation

- Mystical powers: During meditation, the mind's ability to concentrate increases. As a result, man attains various mystical powers like occult powers, healing powers such as *Reiki,* etc. The attainment of such powers strengthens the ego of the individual. Although there are many benefits of these powers, attaining these benefits was not the original purpose of this journey.
- Witnessing extraordinary light during meditation: People feel that seeing some kind of light is the goal of meditation. They do not understand that realizing *that* light in which light and darkness is seen is the real goal. During meditation, if they do not understand anything and experience deep silence, then Silence is the result. But people do not think so. Seeing a light of some kind is perceived as a result. Hence the one who meditates is constantly warned that only seeing something should not become his goal.
- Feeling a lot of strain on the forehead in the beginning: In the quest to attain something, we concentrate our attention and apply strain on the third eye (a spot midway between the eyebrows). Here, the seeker is told, 'Stop seeking and completely lose yourself. Only then will the stress be released.'
- Hope of experiencing the feeling of losing the sense of the body: The answer is that you are not meditating in order to lose the sense of the body. It is true that the feeling of the body is lost during meditation. But you do not need to meditate *in order to* experience this feeling. Whether the sense of the body is lost or not, it

should be of no concern to you. In the pursuit of such an experience, the true purpose of meditation is lost.

- Expecting the result of meditation to be the same every time.
- Meditation done without the right understanding of its original purpose: If this understanding is missing, then meditation becomes 'wasted meditation' (an obstacle to the true purpose).
- Imagination of the experience of 'I'. Truth is beyond imagination. When the mind is unable to see something, it tries to imagine it. Instead of imagining, one needs to just relax and feel it. The prerequisite for meditation is to gain understanding. Otherwise, the mind continues to spin the web of imagination.

Contrast mind – the hurdle in reaching the state of Self Meditation

The biggest obstacle in reaching the state of Self-meditation is the contrast mind[3]. The contrast mind blocks the experience of 'Being' by creating an impression that there is no experience of the Self. Just as the eyeglasses can never see the eyes, similarly, the mind can never know the Experience of the Self. When Bright Understanding is attained, the contrast mind begins to calm down and surrender. Let us understand this obstruction caused by the contrast mind through an example.

The contrast mind is like the weeds that cover the surface of water in a pond, due to which the reflection of the moon is not visible in water. If you want to see the reflection of the moon in the water, it is essential that the weeds be cleared. Even after the weeds are cleared, if the surface of the water is not still due to ripples, the moon appears distorted. Similarly, like the distorted reflection of the moon, the Self too cannot be experienced due to the vagaries of the

---

3. The contrast mind is the comparing and judging mind that labels every experience as good or bad, positive or negative. It lives in duality and is the sole cause of misery in human life.

contrast mind. Various techniques of meditation have been introduced in order to annihilate the contrast mind and reach the stillness of the no-mind state, where the Self can experience itself.

Difference between *Samadhi* and meditation

If you consider meditation from the perspective that it is 'to be done', then meditation is a path and Samadhi is the destination. But if you consider the real meaning of meditation, then 'meditation' is an attribute of the state of *Samadhi* (Self), just as wetness is the attribute of water.

In the beginning, an individual does not know anything about himself. Therefore he is told that you have to practice meditation to reach somewhere, to know something. In this way, the path and the destination are taken as two different entities. Finally, the path itself culminates as the destination. Thus, practicing meditation merely implies knowing your own attribute.

Samadhi is the ultimate goal of meditation. Every session of meditation helps in your progress. It eliminates the beliefs, which act as obstacles in attaining the state of Samadhi. Every time you practice self-enquiry (meditate on 'Who am I?'), you will receive a new direction. A new reality will dawn upon you. Each time, there will be a deeper attack on your wrong beliefs. The conviction that you are not the body will strengthen. The experience of Being will awaken. You will then be able to directly enter into the state of Samadhi.

When there is direct talk with the truth seekers, they are told, 'Meditation is the destination and not the path.' This means meditation is the end in itself, not a means to an end.

SELF WITNESS

Knowing the mind and knowing about the mind are two different types of knowledge. If you want to know *about* the mind, then only the mind can know about the mind.

However, if you want to know the mind, then you will have to detach from the mind and be what you truly are, so as to examine the mind.

You do not have to take help from the mind for this purpose. You have to take the help of the guru. When you look at the world, then the world becomes an object and the eye becomes the knower. However, when you dig deeper, you find that it is the mind that knows the world through the eyes. The eye then becomes the object and the mind becomes the knower. But, when the mind itself becomes the object, then awakens the Self-witness. However, the purpose of the Self-witness is not merely to know the mind or its world. If it merely does this, then it is only being a 'witness'. Its true purpose is to know its own Self. If the 'tongue' is told to taste itself, it cannot do so. But the Self Witness can do this. It can see itself by using the body-mind as a medium, as a mirror, just as the eye needs a mirror to see itself.

The word 'witness' has lost its true significance as it has been used in other contexts. Hence, the term 'Self-witness' has to be used to refer to the true witness.

External sights remind us of the presence of the eyes. Without getting involved with the sights, we should use these sights as a medium to recognize the presence of eyes. Similarly, sound makes us aware that we have ears. Without getting involved in the sounds, return to the ears. Without getting involved with smell, return to the nose. Without getting involved with taste, return to the tongue. Similarly, without getting engrossed in thoughts, we have to know the one who is watching the thoughts, the one who is aware of thoughts, the one who is eternally awake, the one who is knowing. No senses are present there. It cannot be known with the eyes or ears. The external world is merely a reminder or pointer to return onto that ultimate Source. But due to ignorance, owing to lack of understanding, the reminder that we are constantly getting is not received by us. It appears as if that indication is not coming to us. This is the illusion that gets created. Returning onto the Self-witness implies using the external world as a means to permanently abide in the Self.

SELF ENQUIRY

1. 'Who am I?'

There is that 'I' which *people* think you are. There is the 'I' that *you* consider yourself to be. There is the 'I' which you want to become in the future. All these are false concepts. Actually you are beyond all these. You are not what others perceive you to be. You are not what you perceive yourself to be. The one who perceives within you is the real you. Know that perceiver and you shall know the Self or God. You are not to know this intellectually or through words. You can know it only by 'being' it, experientially.

During sleep, you do not feel your body. If there is no body, it means that the senses of the body are also not functional, due to which the world too disappears. On waking up in the morning, you say, "I had good sleep."

But then:

- Who was knowing this in sleep?
- Who was awake?
- Who slept at night? And who remained awake?
- Who awoke in the morning? And who went to sleep in the morning?
- Did it really go to sleep in the morning, or just got concealed by the false beliefs of the mind?
- How do we find that ever-awake witness?
- How do we find the sacred Bright Place (tejasthan) within?
- How to attain that state (which was in sleep) even while in the waking state?

Do contemplate on this. Make the question 'Who am I?' as your meditation.

The body is getting up, sitting, walking, the mind is becoming happy or sad – all this means that you are not the body or the mind. If you are not the body or the mind, then will *you* suffer if something happened to your body or mind? When your pen stops writing, will you get distressed? You will say that the pen has stopped working, let me see what should be done about that. Should it be filled with ink or should the refill be changed? Whatever has to be done, you would not do it sorrowfully. Similarly, whatever is happening is not actually happening with the real you or Self; it is happening with the body and the mind. The seer of the mind is separate and that is who you are. Always remember this.

You are the one who is asking "Who am I?" If you wish to know, "If I am not the body, mind or intellect, then who indeed am I?", then ask yourself, "Who is it that is asking this question?" If you 'know' this from within, then you will get the real answer. 'Who am I' is not a question. It is the answer. People realize this after a long time of sustained enquiry into their true identity. After all, who would want to ask this question? Would the body want to ask, 'Who am I?' It knows very well what it is. Even the mind need not know who it is. The intellect too does not want to know who it is. The one who has the desire to know is the real you. That is why the question should actually be, 'Who is the one who is asking this question?' After attaining the final understanding, when you shall say 'I', then that will be the 'real I'.

If you get the answer to 'Who am I', then what will happen? How would your life be? You have always believed that this body and mind is 'I', but what will happen if this attachment to your body-mind breaks? It would be freedom from all misery. Then even if there is misery, it will be happening with the mind and body; which was happening earlier too.

2. What is the Self?

When the Sun rises, the flowers begin to bloom. Does the Sun do anything for that? People sleeping inside their homes begin to wake up. But the Sun has not even touched them. Similarly, the Self does not issue orders. Orders are passed and carried out by its mere presence.

Everything is inside the Self. Supposing there are different pots inside the ocean. All those pots are inside the water and there is water inside every pot. Likewise there is Self inside each body and all the bodies are inside the Self. There is nothing other than the Self. There is only a curtain in between. The curtain stands for the identification with the body-mind. The Self is on this side of the curtain as well as on the other. There are small and large holes in the curtain. The Self is in them too. Everything is connected. Everything is the Self alone.

The Self was always there and will always continue to be. It is eternal.

3. Why does the Self need a body and a mind?

When the Self is Self, then there is no need for a body-mind. What would your answer be if you were asked the question, 'What is the need for a painter to make a painting?' A painter is making a painting to express himself. Is a painter called a painter after making just one painting? He keeps expressing himself by making many varied paintings. He is creating the paintings for his own joy and for no other reason. His intention behind making these paintings is not to sell them or earn money! All the paintings are the same for him because all the paintings are only indicating towards the one fact that he is a painter. Have you ever seen such a painter who has never made a painting?! No.

Likewise, the answer regarding the requirement of a body-mind is that the Self is 'Nothingness'. The Self wants to express itself in this nothingness. Take the example of a clay pot. When the walls of the pot are made, then there will be empty space inside and outside the pot. Are these two empty spaces different? No, they are one and the same.

Similarly, if we consider the walls of the pot as our body, and if the question is asked: What part of the pot do we use? Do we use the walls of the pot or the empty space inside the pot? The walls of the pot only help in expressing or realizing the empty space. Thus, our essence is the space and not the body.

You say that you were born on a certain date. When you realize that the empty space is the 'real I', then will you say "I was born"? The empty space, which we are in essence, has always been present. When you realize this, you will say, "I have not been born at all." If 'I' is never born, then can 'I' die? Then you are beyond birth and death.

4. Does the mind exist?

The existence of the mind is an illusion. Just as an image in a mirror is an illusion. It exists, and yet it does not. Therefore, we have to understand it. The purpose of understanding is that you get stabilized in the Absolute Silence.

5. How do we reach that state of 'Being'?

There is a fine curtain of the mind that veils the state of 'Being'. When the mind begins to attain understanding that is imparted at the Final Truth Discourses, the curtain disappears. With the fall or surrender of the mind, that state begins to reveal itself on its own. When the ego recognizes the power of God, it surrenders itself. With understanding, it enters into Silence. In that state, there is neither joy nor sorrow. Beyond both polarities is the Supreme Silence, the Bright Happiness.

6. What is Bright Silence?

Bright Silence is the state of absolute silence beyond sound and silence. Words emerge from this silence and disappear into it. This silence exists between every word, between every thought. It is on the paper of silence, that words or thoughts are written. To attain that Silence is to attain the Self.

7. Can understanding be attained through meditation?

No. Meditation is abiding in the Truth within. That Truth is not to be brought from anywhere. It has always been within us and will always be. Attaining the Truth is not difficult. After understanding the false beliefs of our mind, we begin to experience the Truth. Hence, on attaining understanding, it becomes possible to abide in the Truth. Abiding in the Truth is meditation. Thus, meditation follows after understanding has been attained. It is not that meditation is done only sitting at a place. Once understanding is attained, only meditation will remain in every activity – be it sitting, standing, moving around or working.

Hence it is said: Understanding first, meditation later.

Understanding is the seed; Meditation is the fruit.
Truth is the seed; Constant remembrance
of God is the fruit.
First know the truth through understanding.
Then what remains is just meditation
– remembrance of the Lord.

MEDIATION EXERCISES

Technique 1 – Attention on attention

Meditation means doing nothing and also not attending to the task of doing nothing. This is possible only when attention is focused back on itself. It instantly brings you in the present. After reading all the instructions given below, you can immediately begin practicing this meditation.

- For practicing this meditation, sit in a relaxed posture. Look at the scene around you. You may have witnessed it earlier, you will see it now, and see it in the future too. But what will be the difference? Till now, whenever you saw the scene, due to your habit you never looked at it intently, because your mind had already predetermined that you know it - 'I know its name. This is a clock, this is a wall, this is a window, this is a curtain, this is a button, this is a fan' But in this exercise, you should not view things in the same manner as you looked at them earlier. In this meditation, your style of viewing things will undergo a change.

- Look at the things around you as if you do not know the name of anything. This is because when an object is given a name (label), you stop seeing it. When you remove the label attached to an object, you truly begin to see it.
- For any object, if you were to say, 'I don't know the name of this article,' you will find it more vibrant and feel amazed at the sight. Through this exercise, you will see each entity like a child. A child is able to see each object very distinctly, with great interest and joy, because it does not know the name of the object.
- After fully looking at one object, look at the second and then the third. Look at it as though you are not aware of its name. Look at every object and tell yourself, 'I don't know what this object is. I only know that I don't know.' This is called the 'state of bright ignorance,' which means, 'I know that I don't know.' You need to meditate by noticing and asking if the person around you is a boy or a girl. You do not know. Perform this entire exercise with the attitude of not knowing the identity of anything.
- While looking at a scene, pay attention as to where your attention is, from where it slips, from where it gets scattered, and where it gets entangled. Knowing all the aspects about your attention leads to 'attention on attention'.
- After completing the 'open eye' meditation, close your eyes and feel the environment all around you. Is it cold or hot, is there stiffness or lightness in your legs, is

your body tired or sleepy? Feel these things.

- Now open your eyes and look at your body, your hands but do not say, 'This is my hand.' Instead ask, 'What object is this? I don't know what it is.' Only then will you be able to see your body without attachment.
- Close your eyes and feel the detachment towards your body. Feel that you are with the body and not the body. You are 'with the body' means that you are 'a companion of the body'. Observe every sensation that arises in your body with detachment. Apply the same approach to your sensations and say, 'What this sensation is, I do not know.'
- Now with eyes closed, listen to all the sounds present around you. Recognize all the different sounds but do not get stuck on any one sound. Try to detect even the subtlest of sounds. After knowing one sound, move on and try to listen to the next.
- While meditating with eyes closed, observe where your attention gets stuck, from where it slips and where it simply fails to stay.
- With eyes still closed, focus your attention on the thoughts present within you. At that moment, what are the thoughts that are going on? Without labeling them as good or bad, just watch them pass by. Have your thoughts stopped appearing or does a thought say to you, 'There is no thought now.' This too is a thought. Observe it and move on to the next thought.

Remain in this state for two minutes and then open your eyes. You will feel fresh after doing this meditation. What is the state of your attention? Where does it drift? Which objects does it get attracted to and slip away from? In which thoughts does it get stuck? Which thoughts does it chase? Which thoughts does it let go? In which thoughts does it get entangled? You will know all this through this meditation while learning to pay attention to your attention, which is very important.

Through this meditation your thoughts receive the right direction. Aimless thoughts keep appearing for no reason. In this meditation, you have to focus your attention on the present. Be a witness to whatever is happening in the present. Witnessing the witness is to become a self-witness. Hence it is called 'meditating on meditation' - the missing link in spirituality. Becoming a witness of the 'witnessor' means the 'return of attention to the source from whence it emanates'. Only on becoming a witness to the witnessor does real meditation begin. The next meditation further solidifies this experience and understanding.

Technique 2: Complete Meditation

Meditation is complete only when Self observation occurs with awareness. Complete Meditation brings together some meditations seen so far, but at the end of every meditation, you turn within to see who is doing the meditation. When you turn within to ask who is meditating, the mind falls. The mind becomes the boss when consciousness goes to sleep. The mind becomes a servant when consciousness, backed by the strength of Complete Meditation, announces itself as the boss. In Complete Meditation, the Experiencer experiences the Experiencer in and through every experience.

Begin this meditation by following the procedure given below. First read this procedure a few times over to imbibe it fully in your mind. You can also record all the instructions and then play it back.

1. Close your eyes and pray for best results with no expectation that something particular should happen. Then, sit in a comfortable meditative posture.
2. Keeping the body steady, listen to all the sounds around you. Identify at least five different sounds. Do not be in hurry. With a quiet mind, focus your attention on various sounds. Don't get stuck with a particular sound and start listening only to that. Just identify the sound and move ahead.

3. If there is the sound of the rotating fan, then there are other subtle sounds within that sound too. Listen to them attentively. Various types of sounds can include conversations of people, clattering of vessels, children playing or horns and sounds of different vehicles. There can be the sound of something falling, the sound of somebody's footsteps, the sounds of television, music system or radio, the sound of birds or the sound of dogs barking. There can also be the sounds of water flowing, the sound of a whistle or the sound of somebody laughing or crying. When there are no sounds, then try to perceive the sound of silence. Feel the stillness.
4. Try to detect every type of sound around you. If you can hear the sound of an airplane in the sky, then there are different sounds of different types of airplanes. Try to identify the feeblest of sounds. Listen to at least five different sounds - loud, medium or feeble.
5. After having listened to different sounds, ask yourself, "Am I these sounds?" The reply will come from within you: "I am not these sounds; I am the one who is knowing these sounds." Then turn within and see who this knower is, who the ear of the ear is, know the one who is knowing.
6. Now concentrate your attention on the atmosphere. Feel the atmosphere all around you and see whether it is hot or cold, dry or humid, whether the body feels light or heavy, whether there is a swift breeze or a gentle wind, fresh air or less air.
7. If you are able to feel the air, the heat or cold, then ask yourself, "Am I this atmosphere?" A reply will emerge: "No, I am not this atmosphere. I am the one who is perceiving or knowing this atmosphere." Then tell yourself, "Turn around", and know the one who is knowing.
8. Now concentrate your attention on your body. If there is stiffness or pain in any part of the body, just know it

experientially. Do not let the body move even a bit, as far as possible.

9. In the whole body, where lightness or heaviness is felt, where clothes are touching, the air is touching, where itching or dryness is felt, where there is sweating, where there is a burning sensation - feel those parts. This way, notice all the subtle or gross sensations inside and outside the body.
10. Here 'noticing' means 'knowing'. Do not imagine anything; just feel what is happening in or on the body. Do not drive away the feeling of what is happening at present. Do not consider that feeling as good or bad; just feel it as it is. After noticing all the sensations, after knowing what is happening in the whole body, ask yourself, "Am I these sensations?" The reply that will arise will be: "No, I am not these sensations. I am the knower of these sensations." Then immediately turn around and shift to the knower, reach there.
11. Now focus your attention on your breath. Just watch how the breathing is going on. Feel through which nostril you are inhaling and through which nostril you are exhaling. When the breath is going inside, you are aware of the breath going inside. When the breath is coming out, you are aware that the breath is flowing out.
12. Try and concentrate on the breath when it touched the nostrils and the upper lip while inhaling and exhaling. Try and know if the air that goes in and when it comes is warm or cold; know it as as deeply as possible.
13. If your attention goes astray, bring it back to your breathing. Whether the breath went inside silently or with a sound, came out silently or with a sound - perceive that too. Whether the breath is shallow, deep or heavy, however be the breath, keep knowing it without attaching any labels.

14. Whether the breath is coming out through the left nostril or the right, continue to observe this. Ask yourself, "Am I this breath?" The reply will emerge, "No, I am not this breath. I am the knower of the breath." Now know this knower.
15. Now shift your attention from breathing and focus it on the thoughts that arise within. Watch the thoughts that are arising in your mind at this moment. After knowing one thought, know the next thought that arises. There is no need to pursue the previous thought. Just watch a thought and say, "Next." If you get a thought such as, 'No thought is coming at all,' then you have to understand that this is also a thought. After watching this thought, say, "Next." As you go on watching thoughts, you will also feel the joy of detachment from thoughts. Watching all the thoughts that are arising in the mind, ask yourself, "Am I these thoughts?" The reply will arise: "No, I am not thoughts; I am the knower of thoughts." Now know that knower.
16. Now focus your attention on your hands. Know as to how you are feeling in the hands. Now take your attention to your arms and experience how you are feeling there. See whether you are able to feel the arms or not or whether they feel heavy or light. Just know whatever you are feeling. Ask yourself, "Am I these hands?" The reply will appear: "No, I am not these hands, I am knowing these hands." Immediately turn back your attention within and know the one who is knowing these hands. Even if you are unable to know the knower, continue the meditation without getting disappointed.
17. If you are not the hands, then who are you? To know this, take your attention to your legs. See whether you are able to feel your legs or not, whether there is pressure on them or lightness is felt in them. Without putting a label of good or bad, ask yourself, "Am I these legs?" The reply will come: "No, I am the knower of

these legs." Then know that knower. Tell yourself, "I am not the legs." If you are not the legs, then who are you? Ask yourself this question. When you ask yourself this question, don't try to come up with a verbal answer. Just rest in the experience of knowing the knower.

18. Take your attention to the back. See how your back feels. Just know how it is feeling from the shoulders to the waist, whether it is feeling light, heavy, painful or if there is any pressure. Ask yourself, "Am I this back?" The reply will come: "No, I am the knower of this back." Shifting your focus within, know that knower, and tell yourself, "I am not this back."
19. Now bring your attention to your torso and the heart. Continue to know how these parts feel. Ask yourself, "Am I the stomach, am I the heart, am I the neck, am I the shoulders? If I am not any of these, then who am I? I am the knower of all these parts." Immediately shift your attention and know that knower.
20. Now focus your attention on your face. If you are not the torso, then feel your face. See whether you are able to feel your face or not, whether you feel lightness on the face or some sweat on the face. Whether you feel pressure on the eyes or do the eyes feel light, know this. Then ask yourself, "Am I this face?" The reply will come: "No, I am the knower of this face." Shifting your focus, know that knower.

    Tell yourself, "I am not this face, I am not this body, I am not the parts of this body, I am not the breath that is going on in this body, I am not the thoughts, I am not the mind which is just a bundle of thoughts; then who am I? I am the knower of these. I have associated with this body to know who is knowing." As soon as you get this understanding, your attachment to the body will break.

After some time, while remaining in this state open your eyes. After opening your eyes, while still being in the same experience, go outside for a walk. Watch your body walking or working.

Contemplate on the understanding that you gained; the freshness and the internal energy you attained and the shift you received from this experience. Contemplate also on what you learnt and understood from the Complete Meditation. This understanding, this awareness, will transform you and stabilize you in the experience of the Self.

Thoughts testify the Truth

Every action of ours tells us who we consider ourselves to be. Actions arise from thoughts. Our thoughts reflect what we consider ourselves to be. All the thoughts that occur from morning to night are informing us about our presence, our essential existence.

When this understanding deepens, you will be detached from thoughts. You will then behold thoughts in the same way as you would witness fireworks going up into the night sky during festive celebrations. Life would then be a celebration of the truth! When a thought arises, you would say, 'Behold the map of truth!' These very thoughts bear the testimony of the truth, the eternal Presence – the Self. The truth, the state of Silence is the underlying substratum from where thoughts arise.

Thoughts thus testify the truth. Just as sounds testify the presence of ears... sights testify the presence of eyes... odors testify the presence of the nose... the feel of the surrounding air testifies the presence of skin... in the same way, thoughts report your existence, the presence of your Being. These thoughts serve as a mirror to inform: 'I am'. When all your thoughts vanish in deep sleep, you do not realize that you exist. In that sense, it is grace that thoughts arise as soon as you wake up in the morning. When thoughts arise in the morning, they convey the news that you exist; that you are not an animal, but a human – the Supreme Expression of God.

CHAPTER **15**

The world is not as it appears to us; the world is how we are. The only problem lies in seeing others as the problem. What we consider as a 'problem with others' is actually an opportunity for growth.

The path of introspection

The world is our mirror

Why does the world appear as it does to us? Do we all see the same world, or does it appear different to each of us? Whatever be the case, it can be clearly observed that our world appears as we think. Your neighbor may relate to a particular dish with pleasure and enjoy it, while you may find it difficult to tolerate even the smell of the preparation. So, does the problem lie with the dish, or with the way we relate to it?

The world comes into existence when the mind arises, i.e. the world is a projection of the collective mind, comprising the collective thinking processes and belief systems of the entire population. As soon as the mind arises, the world also comes into existence – the world that we consider as 'real'. The world is not plainly what we perceive through our senses. Our perceptions are shaded by our feelings, our past mind programming, our underlying beliefs. It wouldn't be wrong to say that each one of us is carrying our own world within us.

The path of introspection is based on two powerful principles of how we relate to the world:

Principle 1: The world is not as it appears to us; the world is how we think and feel, it is how we are. In other words, the world is a mirror of our own mind.

Principle 2: The only problem lies in seeing others as the problem. What we consider as a 'problem with others' is actually an opportunity for growth, an opportunity to refine our view of the world and in the process explore and rectify hidden quirks of our own mind.

INTROSPECTION

We encounter many problems in our life and become unhappy, but have we ever introspected upon our unhappiness? Have we ever tried to find the root cause of our suffering? If we want to permanently free ourselves from suffering, we need to reach the root of our unhappiness. We should become investigators of our inner truth. As an investigator of the inner truth, we can learn the art of being happy even in unhappy circumstances. To learn how to do this, we need to dive within and explore the depths of our mind. Gradually, we can gain expertise at this. In the process, all the causes of our unhappiness will come to light and disappear.

What happens when a cause is brought to light? Its reality is exposed. Untruth disappears in the light, whereas the truth shines forth. That is how we know what is true. Whatever starts disappearing on coming to light had no existence to begin with. It was just an illusion which had been imprinted in our mind. We had been either nurturing it in ignorance, or had ignored it in our pride and desire for material comforts.

All the unfortunate incidents in life keep recurring so long as we continue with our old outlook. And whenever these situations recur, they make us unhappy. But when our eyes open to wisdom, all the causes of our suffering will come to light. All the events that used to make us miserable will start becoming the cause of supreme happiness. The very people who used to hurt us will become our friends.

When this starts happening to us, it will be an indication that we are becoming adept in introspection. Otherwise, whenever something happens, we promptly stamp it as the truth under the influence of our old outlook. This habit of stamping prevents us from thinking in new ways. It shuts our mind to any other possibility.

In the path of introspection, we utilize the way the world appears to us as a mirror to introspect deeply into the inner workings of our own mind. It is a potent method to encounter our self, to learn more about how we are actually creating our own life situations through the way we think.

For example, if someone complains that his children are disorganized because they throw things around, he would be asked to identify areas where he himself is disorganized. He would be told, "It is fine that you keep all the things in their assigned places. It is great that you remember doing all your tasks. But, look at those areas where you are unable to do this. Do you keep all your thoughts in their assigned places in the cupboard of your mind? Do you do everything according to a schedule? Do you pay regular attention to your heath? Do you use your wealth correctly? Do you shoulder all your social responsibilities? You are careless about so many things; if your children are not perfect in one or two aspects, why must you get so angry? They are your mirror. They are showing you the areas where you commit similar mistakes."

WHAT IS STAMPING?

Stamping means branding something—a person, or a situation according to your own perception. Say you are at work, and a colleague comes into your work area and ignores you. He talks to someone else and leaves. It's such a simple event. There is nothing for you to feel perturbed about; but yet, you feel indignant and hurt. You create a story and stamp it: 'He didn't even look at me—that means he doesn't like me.'

In his ignorance, man keeps creating such stories right from childhood. These stories vary according to his environment, his family's way of thinking and his upbringing. He lives his entire life based upon these make-believe stories.

In the above example, it could very well have been you in place of the individual who ignored you. If you are too engrossed in some urgent or important work, it is likely that you do not pay attention to people around you. That does not mean that you do not like them. But if someone else does the same to you, you immediately make up a story. This fallacy takes root in your mind and imprints unhappiness deep within you.

Stamping is when you pass a judgment about an event, or a person, without thinking rationally, and without knowing the reality. When you give up this habit of stamping or, in other words, when you stop taking your immediate thoughts after an event as the gospel truth, then you will receive a new insight. You will be amazed by the fact that all the events which were the cause of your suffering have become the cause of your joy.

When you keep your prejudices aside and contemplate the event from a new perspective, then the same thing—that you had earlier stamped—reveals its entire existence. All the secrets tumble out and, when the secrets are revealed, you won't remain displeased any more. When you do not know the secrets, you are disgruntled and spread sorrow. Reflect upon what you are spreading and how you look at each event. This investigation will reveal your nature to you.

Say you get shoved by someone, or someone you are waiting for is late, or someone doesn't take your call, steps on your foot while walking, ignores you, boasts in front of you—then your mind starts complaining. That is when you can thoroughly investigate your mind's habitual stamping and how its stories are just that—stories. After a period of investigation, you will reach a point where you will stop having negative feelings about these incidents.

In order to experience this magic in your life, you need

to dig deep into your mind. Then this investigation will become a joy. After your investigation, when you will look at the same incidents again, your root error will come to light. You will wait for such incidents to recur in order to witness your response to them. When you reach such a state, you will experience the bliss of freedom.

INTROSPECTION IN RELATIONSHIPS

Let us understand introspection with an example on relationships.

There was a person who was always very unhappy and worried. One day, he approached his guru for help with his troubles. He told his guru, 'I am fed up of my wife. She never behaves the way I want her to. Regular fights have almost killed the love between us. Is it possible to overcome this situation?'

The guru answered with a question, 'Did you love her when you both were newly married?'

'Of course I did,' the man replied.

'Then why are you having problems with her now? The notion that your wife will behave in a particular manner after marriage is nothing but fallacy—a story contrived by your mind. Think sincerely – Have you married the woman, or have you married your story about the woman? These aspects are so subtle that they don't come to light easily. You need to dig deep within your mind to uncover the reality. Today you are so taken in by your imaginary story that you are unable to accept your life partner the way she is.'

The guru explained further, 'The problem is that man has become a tailor who wishes to fit his customer into the jacket he has tailored regardless of whether the customer is too thin or too fat for it! The tailor keeps waiting his entire lifetime for the customer to fit into his jacket so that he can become happy.

Man suffers because he is adamant that each individual fit into his imaginary jacket. He wants everyone to walk, talk, eat, sleep, laugh and generally behave according to his desire. He wants them to dress according to his taste and be happy in his happiness. Just think and tell me: Is this possible? Every person has a different nature. Somebody may love shopping, but if his partner thinks of it as a waste of money, how can the partner remain happy?

People build their beliefs and expectations around each relationship and, consequently, suffer throughout their lives. Initially, people live together in harmony, but soon they start spinning their own stories about each other in their minds. Thus, the cycle of misery begins.

Everyone expects the other person to change. You let your happiness depend upon whether or not the other person changes. You forget that when you had started the relationship, you had no stories about her. Gradually the stories started forming and the suffering began. Understand this truth and ask yourself in which relations you are attached to your stories.

The irony is that even if someone does fit into your jacket, it doesn't keep you satisfied for long. You tailor another jacket and want that person to fit into this new jacket! In this way, you keep stitching new jackets for people to fit into, so much so that you don't spare even your neighbor, teacher, society or country! Sometimes, your near and dear ones try to fit themselves into your jacket, but you don't remain happy for long because you have developed the habit of stitching new jackets one after another.

If you really want to be liberated from all suffering, you will have to let go of this habit of wanting people to be exactly the way you imagine. You will have to let go of your stubbornness and beliefs about relationships. You will have to accept people the way they are and love them. All this can be achieved only through understanding. No amount of coercion can help here.

Are you ready to free yourself from all the false beliefs and stories that you have accumulated throughout your life?

If you are, then give up all your complaints and start contemplating.

Find out which relationships you have created unhappiness in. Investigate your own thoughts honestly. You have been living with your beliefs and stories for all these years, but they have not helped you in any way. So eliminate them and never let them control your life again.'

The man had been listening to the guru intently. He contemplated upon the words of the guru and understood that he wasn't in love with his wife. Instead, he was in love with his own story about his wife. As soon as he stopped loving his story he realized, 'My wife is just the way she used to be before marriage. I had fallen in love with her the way she was. So why am I creating a new story now and causing both of us to suffer?'

HOW TO INTROSPECT

There are three steps to be followed in the introspection process.

Step 1: Identify the stamping

The first step is to identify what is bothering you. Calmly ask yourself 'what is the exact behavior of the other person that is troubling me'. Form a stamping statement that sums up the upsetting behavior. For example, in the case of the disorganized children, the father can sum up the stamping as 'My children are irresponsible and disorganized'. Take each such stamping statement and go through steps 2 and 3.

The interesting part is that the very moment you identify what is bothering you and consciously refer to it as 'stamping' or 'imaginary story', you begin to dissociate yourself from the trouble and feel better. You open up to the fact that it may not be entirely true and become mentally prepared to search for similar flaws within yourself.

Step 2: Introspect

The second step is the powerful step of learning used to determine where you are repeating the same stamping in various facets of your own life. For example, if the stamping is that 'XYZ is irresponsible and disorganized' or 'XYZ takes me for granted', then you need to throw back the same stamping at yourself and explore all the key facets of your life, such as your physical, mental, social, financial, and spiritual life.

You need to ask yourself questions such as:

- Am I irresponsible in regards to my physical health?
- Do I take my physical health for granted?
- Am I disorganized in my financial planning?
- Do I take my relationships with family for granted?

The key understanding that you need to bear in mind while introspecting is that all the events and life situations that manifest in your life are a mirror of what is happening within you. Thus, if you are unhappy that you never receive help from others, it could mean that you are not helping yourself. If the complaint that arises is that people are rude, it does not necessarily mean that you are rude to others; it could mean that you are possibly rude to yourself!

It is important to analyze how you are repeating the same mistake in all five aspects of your life: viz. physically, mentally, socially, financially, and spiritually. Here are some common complaints and how you can turn it around for introspection:

Stamping	Questions for introspection
Nobody pays attention to me in meetings.	How I don't pay attention to my health? How I don't pay attention to my mental growth? How I don't pay attention to others? How I don't pay attention to my finances? How I don't pay attention to my spiritual growth?
My child is always crying.	How I cry when my body is in pain? How I am depressed when something troubles my mind? How I brood when others don't behave properly with me? How I brood when there is a money problem? How everything I do is equivalent to crying when I am not focused on spirituality?
My brother takes me for granted.	How I take my body for granted? How I take my mind for granted? How I take others for granted? How I take money for granted? How I take my Guru for granted? How I do not accommodate the needs of my body?

My business partner is not accommodating. He is aggressive.	How I am aggressive with myself when I criticize myself mentally? How I am aggressive with others or do not accommodate others? How I am not accommodating with best money practices? How I am not accommodating with consciousness?
My wife blames me.	How I blame my body? How I blame myself mentally and where all I blame myself so? How I blame others? How I blame money for my problems? E.g.: Money is the root cause of all evil.How I blame God when things go wrong?

You have thus seen how you can introspect when any complaint arises in your mind, pointing towards the world. You can be creative in turning around some questions in a way whereby you can introspect deeply. If the stamping is that 'XYZ always keeps crying', then instead of asking 'Do I cry', you can replace the word 'crying' with 'brooding', 'being depressed', 'shouting' etc.

Let us understand how the world mirrors your inner state of mind with another example. Why do you think students who are calm in one teacher's class, bring the roof down in another teacher's class? They answer lies in how the teacher is with herself. The first teacher listens to herself. Automatically, as the world is a mirror, others listen to her. The second teacher is perhaps not committed to herself.

Hence, automatically others do not take her seriously. What is happening outside is a mirror of what is inside. So, when someone takes you for granted, it is a great opportunity for you to dive within and see where you take yourself for granted. Then stop taking yourself for granted.

The second step is not complete by merely seeing the mirror and diving within. The second step is truly complete when you resolve to make-up. When instead of blaming others, you decide to stop doing the same thing with yourself and possibly decide a mental action plan.

Step 3: Re-look and act

The third step is to look at the reality again with renewed understanding and act accordingly. Many seekers who practice introspection have reported that they feel that they are back to a natural happy state at the end of the second stage. Thus, the time is ripe to act clearly from such a happy, natural and clear state.

Any internal change automatically manifests as changes in the external world. Step 3 is all about taking action clearly - without fitting anybody into an imaginary jacket. Step 3 is about seeing reality as it is. Love the reality and act with clarity. In the third step, you need to decide what action you can take regarding your stamping. You may resolve to communicate to the person in question. You may decide not to do anything at all. Or you may decide to wait and watch. But your decision is based on a calm and careful introspection, rather than the impulsive frenzy that arises after stamping.

THE EYE NEEDS A MIRROR TO BEHOLD ITSELF

Whatever you see in the world is just telling you about yourself. Otherwise how will you know yourself? The eye needs a mirror to look at itself. Similarly, man needs a mirror, in the form of relations and events, to recognize the faults within him.

Are you ready to be free from all the false beliefs that you have accumulated over a lifetime? If yes, then give up all your complaints and dive within. Discover how and in which relationship you have been creating suffering for yourself. Enquire into your own thoughts honestly, in a new manner. Become completely free from complaints. Use every complaint to dive within and become clear. Instead of working on others, work on changing how you do the same thing to yourself.

Once you start practicing introspection, the world will not look the same. Gradually, you will come to know that we have come into this world to understand all of this. The world is a wonderful arrangement by itself. It will begin to look more beautiful. You will be able to forgive people without complaining about them. The day you find everyone beautiful and start liking everyone will be the day you have become a good and beautiful person. And then, lo and behold, the world around you will change for the better!

Part-IV

Face of the Supreme Being

The Forms of the Formless

A NOTE TO THE READER

Part IV of the book starts with an elaboration of what Dharma essentially is. All misconceptions and misplaced notions about Dharma in the context of religion and spirituality are expounded in Chapter 16. Missing links in understanding the essence of religion and spirituality are clarified in his chapter.

The remaining chapters in this part predominantly deal with the Indian context; more particularly pertaining to the symbolism of Hindu deities that subtly conveys the message of truth. If you are not familiar with this context, you need not be concerned if you do not understand some of the terms used in this section.

However, the understanding provided in this section has universal relevance. You could apply the same understanding by relating it to your own context. You may experience eureka effect by finding the common thread, the essence that is common to all contexts, be it Indian, American, Egyptian, Islamic, Jewish or any other.

Read this part of the book, particularly to understand the chapter where the '*The New Temple of Today*' is explained with an effective analogy of a single-bladed fan.

CHAPTER 16

The essence of religion

Rituals are wrappers that convey true spirituality

We start using whatever we understand. When we understand the body, we start using the body; when we understand the mind, we start using the mind. However, if we do not use them, they start using us. The mind uses us, the body becomes our master. With time, every belief dominates our life. Due to such beliefs, our life is dominated by the individual ego amidst people and end this lifetime in discontentment. If we make corrections to these aspects of our life, we gradually start establishing ourselves in our dharma (essential nature).

In this chapter, we will address the questions on religion and spirituality. There are various questions that have been put up regarding the prevalent beliefs and concepts of religion, spirituality, and rituals. The answers to these questions cut through preconceived notions and unearth the missing links to unresolved aspects on this topic.

1. Why was dharma started and by whom?

A: The belief inherent in this question is that dharma did not exist earlier and then someone came later and started it. This is as if whoever started it came first and dharma came later. So who can have the power or capability to start dharma? dharma alone starts dharma. To understand this, you will need to understand what the word 'dharma' is being used to refer to. The word dharma is used in two contexts. Whatever is used in two contexts becomes adharma (apart from one's true nature); it is then no longer beneficial. People use such words as they want depending on the situations. The word dharma has been used in 2 different ways. Just like the word 'Atma' which is used to refer to the subtle body as well as to refer to the Self. Due to this, such words have been misinterpreted and have led to a lot of delusion. Till today, people are still stuck in this confusion and misunderstanding. So these old words need to be either abolished or then it is necessary to explain the essential meaning of such words. The solution to this delusion can come only if such words are used in a single context. Otherwise, so many questions arise on such words and clarity seems far from sight. Let us understand what dharma is.

A box containing a pen is kept before you. If someone asks you what this box is, you would say, it is a pen. You say it easily because it is obvious to you. But you should also realize that it is not a pen. It is only after opening the box that you get to the pen. Similarly what people are calling as dharma is not really dharma. Dharma is obtained only after opening the parcel. The biggest fallacy and hurdle in spirituality is that people assumed the parcel to be dharma. You know that the parcel is not the object that it is used to wrap. You should definitely make use of the packaging, it has its own benefits. However, if the parcel itself becomes so decorative and attractive, people get lost in it. So it can lead to such a great misunderstanding, and hence it is very important to understand how dharma has been used in two different contexts – for the parcel as well as the essence that is inside the parcel. If the word pen was used to represent the box containing it, people will take the box and say that they have a pen, even though the box may be empty. The parcel may be empty, but people may be in the fallacy that they are having dharma with them. So, people keep blindly following rituals and claim that they are following dharma. They vow that they will never leave their dharma. They need not leave it, but they need to first see whether that pen writes (functions). In order to see whether it writes, they will have to open it first. When they open it, they will find that the real essence is not at all inside it. So with the passage of time, it becomes necessary to address this fallacy. The question was who started dharma. No one can start dharma, because it was there from the very beginning. First comes dharma, the packing can be started later by someone, so that such an important thing is not just kept as it is, it is wrapped carefully. Let people understand its value. Otherwise, no one values such an important thing that we have obtained by default. Just like the experience of the Self, that is there with us by default. Just like sunlight, or oxygen which is obtained by default, its value is lost. Similarly dharma was also obtained by default; the child is born and it is told that it belongs to this particular dharma. Hence, there remains no value for that. So to re-remember the value, people can start with the packing. Otherwise, dharma refers to the state of God. The world was created later. Wherefrom the world was created exists from the very beginning. Then the world became visible. The original state. The word dharma refers to the original state. The word dharma refers to nature. To make something effective, a good packing is required. So no one can start dharma, dharma alone is the alpha and omega. There is no question of there being a beginning or end of dharma. But people, who can understand it later and want to raise its value will add certain things around dharma to give it value. People may get lost in the surrounding aspects that are added around it and call that dharma. Just as the mistake of referring to the box of a pen as a pen can always occur. It is this fallacy that gives rise to such questions.

2. What is the purpose of dharma?

A: Dharma itself is the purpose. When people do not understand the real meaning of dharma, they are bound to design such questions. Who are you? If you are the body, then whatever happens with the body becomes you nature. In the body, blood flows, thoughts are flowing, breath is ongoing. Diseases can go on in the body. One can observe something or the other going on in the body every moment. So all this can be misinterpreted to be our nature. But it is not your nature. The instrument that you are using, the pen that you are using, if some thoughts arise in that pen, you clearly know that these thoughts are arising in this pen, which help in creating words. This is why words have been placed in the pen. So that while writing, we need not write the entire word. When we write the word "We", we will have to write both the characters – "W" and "e". But, if such an arrangement has been already made in the pen, then the moment you write "W", the next character "e" will be automatically written by the pen. So why is this arrangement done? So that you can express yourself fully. So thoughts are given to the body, so that your time is not wasted. Something has already been filled in the body from the beginning. However, the thoughts of the pen create pain, because such words arise that are unnecessary. So then trouble will be felt in erasing those; effort will be required to do so. If you don't know how to use the pen (body-mind), then such thoughts will arise that give pain. You need to learn how to handle the pen, how to hold it. How to understand dharma, how to hold dharma. You hang dharma on a hanger and claim that you are Hindu, or Muslim, Sikh, or Christian. The dress is on the hanger. If you never wear it, you will never get the feel of it. The feeling of wearing comes when we remove it from the hanger and wear it. So how is the pen to be held? When we understand and embrace dharma in its essence, then the purpose of dharma gets fulfilled. Dharma is the purpose in itself, if you are able to understand this definition of dharma that it is the essential nature, dharma itself is the nature of God, then embracing it, wearing it will become very easy. You will then be able to identify with this purpose and work towards fulfilling it. Otherwise, you would never feel this to be the purpose. This purpose gets fulfilled when you know the nature of who you truly are, and seize the opportunity to express your true nature. All this is merely a field of activity. In this field, the tasks assigned to various people are merely a pretext. Everyone has been assigned a field of activity. The ultimate purpose has to be fulfilled in this field of activity. So, to align with your true nature, you need to understand your true nature and also realize at the earliest that you are not the body and start living in the conviction of this realization – this will be the purpose.

3. Is dharma eternal, immortal?

A: If you understand dharma in the right context, then the answer would be Yes. dharma is eternal, it is immortal. If you consider dharma to be the external cover, the packing, then you know that some packaging ends up in the dustbin, while certain others are retained carefully. The packaging here refers to religious beliefs and rituals. So the packing is not eternal. Dharma, which is understood in its true context, is eternal.

4. Does dharma depend on any particular belief-system, doctrines, or sect of society?

A: It's exactly the other way round! Belief-systems, doctrines, and sects in society depend on dharma. Anything that has to sustain needs something in the centre, something permanent, around which it revolves, based on which it functions. If there is something in the centre, then this becomes possible. For example, for a fan to function, you would need to fix it's centre. If the rod to which the fan is attached and the ceiling were also to rotate, then the fan cannot function. Something has to be fixed first. Then civilization or social order can be founded upon this fixed base. You got to have faith on something that can never change. You can have faith only on that which is changeless, that which is fixed. This fixed principle is dharma. So, the answer is exactly the other way round.

5. Is dharma different from nature? Is it primeval or original (without anything else before it)?

A: Dharma is primeval and eternal. Regarding the difference between dharma and nature, nature is the manifest form of dharma. Something that is formless attains a form. Form is a manifestation, an expression that occurs due to the presence of something. Expression through form is due to the presence of the fundamental principle, which is formless. Without the existence of the formless, form cannot come about. Dharma is formless and its presence cannot be experienced until it is given an instrumental form. Nature is the manifest form of dharma. Nature enables you to experience or feel the presence of dharma. Again, this is possible only if the person is sensitive. Dharma is the fixed eternal formless presence which causes flowers to blossom, rivers to flow, stars to shine. What is that thing for which it can be said that owing to the presence of this thing, everything has come about! If this thing was not there, then all this creation wouldn't have been. When people sing songs such as, 'Everywhere it is your celebration!', it was based on this understanding that its manifest form is being seen in nature. Dharma has become manifest as Nature. This is why some people like to refer to God as Nature.

6. Is dharma defined by man?

A: Dharma is not defined by man; on the contrary, man is the instrument to realize dharma. Man can never define dharma. If you consider the other definition of dharma (as the packaging), then the packaging is indeed defined by man. But if we are discussing the real context of dharma, then man is merely an instrument; the human body is the only medium through which dharma can experience itself. Man is the medium or the mirror meant for this purpose; the mirror cannot define dharma.

7. What is the relationship between sacred places of pilgrimage and dharma?

A: When people realize that something is important, then a place needs to be established. For example, if you come to know that a particular thing will be of immense use to everyone, like garments, electronic goods, or furniture, then you establish a place, like an electronic market or furniture market. This is because you came to know that people need these things, and let there be a place meant for these commodities. When you visit a shopping mall, you find particular types of shops located at the same place. Why are all these shops co-located? So that it becomes convenient for people, they can easily shop. All these things have been arranged to make it convenient. In addition to these benefits, such as convenience, the vibration of the place starts becoming typical. In the place that you visit, if people of the same type keep visiting that place, then the vibration of that place becomes more and more typical for those people. If you go and sit in the meditation room, then this room is visited by those who have meditation as their sole purpose. The vibration of the meditation room contributes to make the atmosphere more amenable for meditation. If this goes on for many years, then that place develops such a vibration, such purity, which helps newcomers attune to the environment easily. So that people can experience their true nature as soon as possible at that place. People who have faith in dharma will visit such sacred places of pilgrimage. Religious people will get attracted to such places. It's a different story that with the passage of time, ritual-mongers start advocating and recommending various rites and rituals, making it commercialized, due to which the vibrations of those places begin to become corrupt. Just as even sacred rivers like the Holy Ganges become corrupted due to the contamination of the waters, similarly it happens with such places of pilgrimage. But those who established such sacred places, did so in order to cater to people who visit with this purpose, just like people visit the electronic market to explore the latest advancements in the world of electronic appliances. Why do people visit the Kumbh Mela in India? It is because they would meet those people who are engaged in their sadhana (spiritual practices). People who are thirsty for the truth would congregate at such places. There has to be some arrangement where people can congregate and learn. So depending on the kind of seeker, they would get an appropriate guru. Each one's requirement will be fulfilled. Why are all cloth shops found in the same place? So that whatever the need may be, that should be fulfilled by visiting one place. People who established such places did so with foresight, so that such establishments should not just benefit the current generation, but also many future generations to come. With the pretext of a festival, or religious event, or pilgrimage, when people come and explore what is available, only then can they pray for such things in their lives. They will be able to ask themselves whether they too can live frugally. When we see certain people leading a given way of life, we are inspired to live that way. But when indolent and lazy people start acting like sages, they cause harm to people around them. But to say in short, the purpose of such sacred places of pilgrimage was indeed grand. Those who were focused on benefits are deriving benefit even today, while those who are prone to delusion are getting deluded. So it is essential to re-think upon the purpose of such sacred places.

8. What is the difference between Nature, Dharma, God, and Science?

A: God, Dharma, Nature, and Science. If we want to differentiate between these, then God's nature is Dharma; Nature is the manifest expression of dharma, and the laws of Nature that have been understood are called Science. So science is discovering the laws of Nature. Science keeps unraveling secrets of how Nature functions. So the difference between these shows how the various aspects of the one underlying principle are interlinked. They all are in the same flow. Some things are such that if you understand them, then you would have understood everything.

9. What is the relation between dharma and spirituality?

A: In the context of this question, when people talk about dharma, they are considering it to be religion, the packing, and hence this question arises. They consider dharma to be various religions such as Hinduism, Islam, Christianity, Sikhism, Buddhism etc. So then what is spirituality? Spirituality is that form of dharma that is lived, that which is brought into living. It is the form of dharma that is embraced in daily life. Hence, some people have said, don't talk much about dharma; practice it! This was said because people have assumed dharma to be a particular religion, the belief that those who perform these particular rituals belong to this separate religion. Such religionist people become stubborn and uncompromising on their belief-systems about religion; they haven't understood that those beliefs have nothing to do with real dharma, it is to do with the packaging around it. Some people become stubborn and say I want to receive dharma in this plate only; I don't want it in any other form. There are people who carry their plate wherever they go, even on picnics. Some people carry their pillow wherever they go, as they do not get sleep with any other pillow. They are fixed about using that pillow, and cannot adapt to anything else. They do get the place to sleep, but they can't do without their fixed pillow. Similarly, there are some stubborn religionists who want dharma to be served in their own terms, in their own plate. They will say that we want these specific words to be used. And there are some who used to ask, 'why are you inventing new words, why don't you use words that already exist in the Vedas, in scriptures. Why are you starting this anew?' So there are such people who have studied Vedas to such an extent. They know all the words used in the scriptures. They don't understand what is the need in today's society, in today's language. Accordingly certain words will be coined so that it becomes true spirituality and is embraced into practical living. Let it be practically used. Spirituality (Adhyatma = Adhi + Atma, in Sanskrit) refers to the state the Self before it came into action. But the belief-systems of creeds or sects are assumed to be dharma. Some people become spiritualists, while some become religionists. This is because the two are assumed to be different. But in truth, the essence of dharma has to be embraced in practical living. This is why the word 'spirituality' was coined. Spirituality is pure, hence people would say, 'Don't be religious; be spiritual.' This is like saying "Be Indian, not Hindustani". The one who understands this will clearly see that what's being said is meaningless; the one who is saying this does not understand what he is talking. So casting aside the packing such as specific words and rituals belonging to a particular creed or sect, new words will be coined so as to focus on the pure essence of spirituality. Spirituality contains the word 'spirit', referring to the original state of the Self that came into action. When you understand this process that whatever I am experiencing right now is in a state of action through the body, then how should this action be in this world? How to respond in this world? The one who knows his true identity, his original nature in and through every response, is spiritual. Those who follow rites and rituals are religionists. This distinction was created. But you now understand this in the right context that dharma is your essential nature, that alone has to be applied, and that alone has to be brought into action.

10. Which religion's prayers are fulfilled sooner? Christians have more faith in prayers; so then do their prayers get fulfilled sooner?

A: This question arises from the system where it is told that if people belong to this particular religion, then their prayers are fulfilled faster. People of this religion will attain heaven; the remaining will go to hell. People want such shortcuts. In the same way, in spirituality, the same belief has been rampant with gurus; the belief that if you follow this particular guru, then your place in heaven will be confirmed. People who dwell in such shortcuts do not do anything in life to be truly spiritual. Just by chanting the name that their guru has assigned for them, they feel that their seat in heaven is confirmed! They then get their family members to also practice the chanting of this name and believe that their seats will also be confirmed. So such shortcuts come into being. Similarly, with dharma, people ask in which religion prayers are fulfilled faster, so that they can then embrace that particular religion. People of certain sects even declared that people from other sects, like those who follow idol-worship, are worshipping the devil and will go to hell. This is because they decided to believe that idols are forms of the devil. They even wrote these beliefs into their religious tenets. Even those scriptures that were pure to begin with underwent many rounds of so-called correction, in the process of which, whoever edited these works added their own personal flavors into the scriptures. They did so to achieve their political ambitions of increasing their followers in the world, so that their sect, their religious creed can dominate the world. When people hear such biased perspectives, 10% people who think rationally will not fall into such traps, but 90% of the masses who do not reason, get lured by such hollow claims. These advocates of religious creeds continue their propaganda to entice this 90% of the masses. Those who can understand and reason, will question such baseless claims. But others fall a prey to such beliefs in their childhood. They feel nice when they are told that they belong to a certain religious sect and hence are superior. When you are using a particular brand of toothpaste and see the same advertisement on television, you feel reassured and satisfied that you are going in the right direction. You find that you are using the same soap that is being advertised in the media, you become glad that you are associated with that soap. Similarly when they hear that the religious sect to which they belong has more followers, they are pleased. They are delighted to know that people in their sect will attain heaven. They never try to reason or assess the authenticity of what they are being told. If people live unconsciously and perform deeds without thinking, how can they attain their so-called heavens!? Even if such people reach their imagined heavens, they are actually hells. Because they imagine heavens that are overflowing with fountains of wine, various forms of entertainment. Their tendencies are still so strong during their lifetime on earth that they wish to continue with the same vices even in heaven. Even if they attain such a heaven, they do not even realize that have actually chosen a worse hell. Such a gross misunderstanding! So when you look at what's going on with the right understanding, true dharma is not at all based on any belief system or religious sect. It is not at all the case that the prayers of people from this particular religious faith will yield more effective or quicker results. This rather depends on the inner state of mind of the person; it depends on the person's level of clarity. Let him belong to any religious faith or belief system, if he is clear and not doing contradictory prayers i.e. if his prayer is single-pointed, if his prayer has intense feeling, and there's a vacuum created within him to receive whatever he is praying for; when he calls out from a feeling of helplessness, then the prayer gets fulfilled. Prayers are never fulfilled externally. It is all about the internal state of mind. When vacuum is created in here, then the air from outside has to rush in. Regardless of which religion you belong to, if such a state of receptivity is created within you, the prayer is bound to be fulfilled, often in miraculous ways. Not because you follow any particular religion, but because of your inner clarity. There are certain rituals that help in increasing the focus and concentration for prayers. But the fulfillment of prayers is not dependent on those rituals. It all depends on the inner state of feelings, inner wisdom, faith, love, the intention behind praying; all these drive the fulfillment of prayer, regardless of whatever religious beliefs are being followed. Why is it believed that the prayers of children are easily fulfilled? It is because children pray with inner purity of mind. The child prays without attachment with doubtless faith on the father. Some arrangements can be made to help make the prayer effective. For example, when people agree to pray together for a common cause at a common fixed time, say 09:09AM or 09:09PM, this is merely an arrangement so that people from around the globe can pray together. One can make such arrangements taking the timings of various countries into consideration, so that those who can offer prayers can do so at the decided time, and those who need help from mass prayers should be able to receive at the same time. Whoever is going through pain or trouble, will be seated in a mental state of receptivity so as to receive the effects of prayers being offered by people at the given time. This state of receptivity brings forth the needed result. External methods can definitely help, but to believe that a certain method alone is the best is wrong. This is because it is easily seen that with any religious belief-system, there are still cases where prayers are not fulfilled, there are still sinners, there are people steeped in ignorance, regardless of which religion they belong to. Wherever, an intense need arises, things start flowing into the inner vacuum that is created. This functions relentlessly by natural laws, regardless of which religion the person belongs to. Whether the person is praying consciously or unconsciously, the results are bound to come.

11. Why are people who abide by religion or follow rituals considered fanatic or foolish?

A: It is not necessarily people who abide by religion or follow certain rituals that are considered foolish. Whoever does something new in any field of activity is considered foolish to begin with. If someone does something altogether different from prevalent norms, then it is likely that he will be considered foolish. People normally follow certain routine after waking up. But, if someone does something different, he will be called a fool. This is because it does not fit into the collective norms of approved behavior; people tend to follow a fixed framework. The training for conditioned conventional thinking begins from our schools. In many schools, it is seen that scoring is based on a fixed framework. Students can score well only if they write answers in a particular way. There are children who can solve arithmetic problems using their own intuitive method; however they are not awarded good scores as their method is considered to be outside the approved methods decided by the system. They are considered foolish, just because they resort to new methods of solving the same problem. There are children who can solve arithmetic questions visually by merely looking at the numbers, without using any logical formulae. Although they are able to successfully solve complex problems visually, they are still forced to follow conventional methods. They can score only if they follow systematic formulae. As a result, during the formative years, people who are forced to follow conventions, become trained to be conventional and rigid, so as not to displease their teachers and parents. With this background, even after growing up, the person remains conventional and goes against his natural intuition. When he hears something different, say he hears someone pronounce words in a given way, he gets angry as he is trained to pronounce in a conventional way. This is because he has been trained to live and think within a limited framework since childhood. When one is willing to re-learn, he will introspect and question every belief that arises from within into his conscious awareness. Such people who are willing to question old limiting beliefs and embrace the new are also labeled foolish by society. People who are following spirituality or religion are considered foolish as they are seen as being un-scientific or unconventional. It is not just with spirituality or religion, but with anything new that challenges prevalent norms. Anything that deviates from the current fashion is considered bizarre or eccentric. This is natural. Man needs to think and question prevalent beliefs at least with those things where there is no sense in blindly imitating conventions. Even if people consider it foolish, one must resolve to continue embracing the new. One must try and explain why they are trying something new and communicate to those who do not approve of it in ways which they can understand. When you are firm about your decisions and continue whatever you are doing despite being criticized, then slowly you will find that people will begin to support you.

12. Why are people who follow a lot of rituals believed to be more religious?

A: There's a difference between knowing and believing. Man's reach is limited to the world of forms; he cannot easily grasp the formless. Someone who does a final truth retreat understands the truth, but it has not translated into action in his life as yet. People will be quick to point out that he has not benefited from the retreat. The person may claim that he has benefitted from the retreat, since he no longer feels depressed as he used to feel before the retreat owing to his ignorance. People will accept that he has been benefitted from the retreat only when they are able to see tangible results such as worldly success, harmonious relationships as an outcome of the happiness that he is experiencing. Without tangible results, people cannot see the benefits due to their inability to grasp the unseen. Hence, rituals were given more importance. There are many people who believe that it is more important to appear good, rather than actually being good. Similarly people do the reverse. They perform rituals to appear religious, rather than actually being religious or spiritual. Being spiritual is difficult for them, since they do not want to attend to truth discourses. They do not want to introspect and contemplate on the truth. It is much easier for them to follow rituals so that people in their community will be impressed and respect them. When they follow rituals, their society starts valuing them. As a result, rituals started becoming popular as an external demonstration of religion. Whatever we strongly feel within, naturally shows up in our actions, but it is also possible to put on an outward act to pretend an inner feeling. When some people really started experiencing happiness by abiding in the truth, they started naturally expressing that happiness by following certain customs, like folding their hands in obeisance to the sun. The feeling within such people is that of gratitude arising from the understanding that God is everywhere; they will love and celebrate everything around them. Folding hands, singing divine hymns, dancing in divine ecstasy are merely a natural external expression of what they were experiencing within. Seeing all this, society started making this into a formula that those who are religious are supposed to fold hands in obeisance, sing hymns, dance, etc. The original state was the experience of Self around which all these forms of expression got associated. People started practicing these forms of expression ritualistically even though they had no experience of the Self within. These rituals were then made as a reminder for them to abide in the Truth. The act of applying vermillion (*Tilak* in Hindi) on the forehead was with the intention of remembering the truth of life. Seeing each other wearing vermillion was meant to serve as a mutual reminder of the truth. These arrangements for reminding the truth later turned into blind rituals. Ashrams and temples were created so that people can visit such places and contemplate upon the truth. A special place meant for this purpose would raise the possibility of seeking for the truth. However, visiting such places of worship then became a mechanical ritual and people who followed rituals such as visiting temples or reading scriptures were labeled as 'religious'. The practice of reading the scriptures a fixed number of times evolved as a practice to increase the focus and concentration of the mind. However, this practice also turned into a ritual, as a result of which, people who were experts in reciting the scriptures were considered as being religious. This is because all these external expressions are visible. Whatever is visible can be remembered. This is the limitation of human memory. The idol representing Lord Shiva is a visible symbolic form of the truth (we will understand this more elaborately in the next chapter). The features of the idol of Shiva are meant to remind of the various aspects of the truth, of higher wisdom. When aspects of truth are associated with a form, the form becomes a packaging that helps as a medium to carry these aspects as a message to future generations. But then people forget the essential meaning or message inherent in these symbolic forms and get stuck in rituals, literally considering the idols to be God. Again, this is because whatever is visual is more effective, it is more easily remembered. Rituals are visible; hence it becomes easier to relate to them. The gesture of acceptance is a visible symbol of the understanding of true acceptance. The symbol makes it more effective and possible to remember. If it were not for this symbol, many people would not have derived as much benefit from the teaching of acceptance. This is the reason why people who perform rituals are considered more religious. Those who pretend by following rituals will also be considered religious.

13. What religion does an atheist (non-believer of God) belong to?

A: A non-believer belongs to the ABCDE religion. 'A' for Agyan (ignorance), 'B' for Behoshi (unconsciousness or stupor), 'C' for confusion, 'D' for Dukh (sorrow or depression), and 'E' for ego. He is ignorant about what the word 'God' really refers to. A philosopher called Nietsche stated that God is dead. This statement became very popular. God is life itself; the enlivening principle, consciousness due to which everything exists and is experienced. So if one says that God is dead, it is like saying that life is dead. If life was to die, then one wouldn't be present to even make this statement! The very living act of making this statement itself proves that God is still alive. He may be right according to the meaning of the so-called God that he held in his mind. Many children are silenced by giving fears about horrifying characters. They are told that they should behave properly, else such fearsome characters would appear before them. However, when they grow up, they come to know that such characters never existed. They may then state that these characters are now dead in their life. But the fact is the characters, as they understood them, never existed. That image can be dead. A coat that is hanging in the dark may appear like a thief. When you go closer, the so-called thief vanishes. In reality, the thief was never there from the very beginning. So Nietsche may have talked about the 'so-called' god, the image that he had conceived in his mind, which never existed in truth. If he had understood the real meaning of God, he would never have made that statement. When people forget the real meaning, then they start valuing his statement in a literal sense. How can life be dead when you are alive and talking? Life is going on. Life was always there from the very beginning; the human body came later as an expression of life. When water collects in puddles during the rainy season, insects start breeding there. The fetus comes into being in the mother's womb and starts breathing because life was there in that space from the very beginning. God or life is present even in the space between bodies. Life alone is. Everything that appears is happening inside life, inside God. The word God can be misleading to some people. In western countries, people avoid using the word God. They prefer to use the word Self, as they have a different belief-system about God. There is no need to get entangled in words.

One may use the word God or Self, it really doesn't matter. What God refers to needs to be understood. God refers to Life, the enlivening principle, consciousness, that due to which everything is. People who do not understand this meaning will continue to make statements that God does not exist. It's due to ignorance that he becomes non-believer. When someone attains wisdom he becomes a Bright believer – one whose faith does not shake in any situation or scene, one whose faith in God is unconditional. This is because even so-called believers in God, are actually non-believers so long as they do not understand God in essence. Their faith keeps vacillating like a pendulum! A few difficult situations in life can shake the faith out of him. His faith oscillates like a pendulum subject to the fulfillment of his desires. So, both are non-believers. Believing and non-believing are two faces of the same coin. One face is hidden at the time when the other is visible. In testing situations, the believer can become a non-believer, or even the other way round. They have not done their homework. They blindly conclude without introspecting or contemplating upon this. This happens due to ignorance and unconsciousness. On what basis do people say that they do not believe in God? Have they every researched on this topic before making such tall statements? And even those who claim that they believe in God, even they do so without having actually researched and contemplated upon what they really believe in. Such blind beliefs stem from the conditioning since childhood where the child is influenced by opinions of people around him. He needs to introspect what God really is. He needs to ponder why some people believe in God while others do not. What is the reality? He needs to understand the topic in depth before deciding whether God exists or not. Without contemplation, there is bound to be confusion, as one keeps moving between believing and not believing. The lack of belief in God also stems from sorrow that has been experienced in life. Ego also leads to lack of belief in God. Ego gives rise to the tendency of taking credit for whatever is achieved. There is a sense of doership due to which one cannot surrender to the presence of the unseen living force that enables everything. When one gets rid of ignorance and unconsciousness, one would say that regardless of who gets the credit, I should know the truth. Let the credit be mine or God's, it does not matter; it's more important for me to know the truth. The one who thus falls in love with the truth alone can have Bright unconditional faith.

14. Why do different religions follow different rituals? Are rituals a part of religion?

A: Different religions follow different rituals. Hindu rituals are different from those followed in Islam, which is still different from what Christians follow. Rituals are created as an arrangement depending on the times when the need for these rituals came up, the moods of people, the weather of the geographical location, prevalent social conditions and beliefs of the place where the religious faith came into being. In a situation where people are uneducated or unavailable to reason, a different set of practices or rituals are associated. Rituals are created depending on the immediate need of the given time and place. This was because it was clear to the messengers of truth that depending on the needs of each era, bodies will be prepared to guide the masses depending on the needs prevalent at that time. With the availability of recording systems in modern times, the possibility of ensuring that the right message reaches people has significantly increased. In olden days, such recording systems did not exist. So the constant focus of people who can guide has been on where people are stuck today. What are their limiting beliefs that are preventing them from experiencing the truth? What arrangements can be made so that they will feel the need to be in the experience of the Self? These aspects have been taken into consideration while designing spiritual practices or rituals. These practices or rituals differed because the weather is hot in some places, while it is cooler at other places. In hot places, rituals involving fire will be avoided as it is already hot. It is just like the practices followed to dispose dead bodies in various geographical places. These became the practices of various religions. For example, in hot places like deserts, bodies were buried, not burnt as it is already so hot, and it is difficult to find firewood in the deserts. In green agricultural terrain, it was easier to consign the body to flames by using firewood, as wood was aplenty and space was limited. So the basic clarity was that depending on the need that arises, accordingly the body can be buried, or burnt, or fed to birds. Depending on need, different practices came into being. However, one who sees these differences without this understanding would believe that these are different religions. But with the thread of understanding that binds all religions together, it will become clear that one and the same dharma is being referred to. It is just that various other aspects were associated around the dharma depending on the needs of the times and the place. There are many rituals which are not required today. Yet people follow it because they have been seeing people around them doing the same since their childhood. We can choose to continue those practices which we need today; and get rid of those practices that we no longer need. We can use our creativity to bring new ways that are more applicable to the current context to realize the truth. So due to this reason, rituals may appear different. Very often rituals are designed depending on the desires of people. Those who wish to have a feast of meat will design rituals of animal sacrifice. Depending on the weather, if it is winter, then people will prepare sweets using fat and sugar for winter festivals. Many such things get associated with dharma. With the right understanding, one would never hate or criticize any religion or claim superiority. You would say that rituals are merely an arrangement, a packaging for dharma.

15. Why is the younger generation staying away or moving further apart from religion?

A: Because the old generation has already moved away from religion. If they had not moved away, it would have been transferred. Children begin to believe and experience whatever their parents believe and experience. If parents merely follow rituals blindly and mechanically, children see that these rituals have not really resulted in any positive benefit to their parents. They are still leading a life of struggle, unhappiness, disharmony, and discontentment. And yet parents claim to be religious. Seeing this, children question the worth of such religion in their own lives. Due to this they lose faith in religion and even begin to hate spirituality. Attending truth discourses is considered old-fashioned or futile for this reason. Some children who are avid readers are teased by their classmates, who call them 'bookworms'. Likewise, those who attend truth discourses are also teased as being old-fashioned or weird. Children focus on superficial beliefs that are formed by their generation. They do not focus on what benefit can come from true spirituality. Everyone wants true and lasting peace and happiness, which is the essence of spirituality. If parents were truly happy and experiencing their essential nature, it would have naturally been expressed in their thoughts, words and action. How many parents today are able to tell their children that their body likes a particular dish? How many parents refer to their body separately with the clarity that they are not the body-mind? Do children hear their parents saying "Today my body is paining (I am not paining)?" Parents should form this habit after realizing the truth. If children clearly hear this distinction between their body-minds and their essential nature from their parents in their childhood, then they will never stay away from dharma. They would remember that any pains are with their body-mind, they would remember their true nature, their dharma. Children who watch their parents being happy and stable in and through the trials and tribulations in life will be able to easily grasp and establish themselves in dharma. They will emulate their parents who lead by example. They will be able to say that their parents gave them this wealth of true wisdom. The old generation is already far away from dharma since ages! Hence the new generation is moving farther away. People are keeping dharma alive through rituals. Someone needs to unearth and explain the true meaning and purpose of these rituals and idols and point to the real essence behind everything. The parcel of religion in the form of rituals and mythological stories has reached the younger generation. However, the message of opening the parcel and experiencing what lies within needs to be given to them. The very purpose of the parcel was that when the parcel reaches the future generation, someone would open the parcel. But no one is opening the parcel; they are merely worshipping the parcel. It is like being seated in front of the television without switching it on. The very purpose of the television is lost if it is never switched on. Similarly, the very purpose of rituals and practices is lost if one does not go beyond the rituals to access the real purpose behind them. Only when one uses the parcel to understand the essence that is hidden within will religion become a living aspect of life.

16. Why do only depressed or troubled people believe in religion or God?

A: This is a very common belief that only those who are troubled and depressed embrace spirituality. Due to this belief, those who appear to be happy feel that they do not need spirituality. This is far from the truth. Some people believe that sick people need to visit the doctor. This is true. Some there can be people who want to be always healthy, who would visit the doctor to know how to maintain good health. And there are also those who aspire to be future doctors; they also visit the doctor! Some people aim to be always in service of humanity, they work for a cause larger than their personal needs. So then they would choose how they can be of service. Depending on how trained your body-mind is, you would choose an area of service accordingly. If you are not very well trained, you will chose a basic way of serving. If you are highly trained, you will choose to serve in a significant way. After attaining self-realization, one would choose that service which is not being attended to at all, where no one is focusing, but which is urgently needed. So one who is able to clearly see and appreciate the urgency will naturally take up to the task. There are many avenues through which service can be rendered. And yet, if people are unaware of the need, then who will take up the onus to start? It is after self-realization that one can clearly see the needs and understand the level of training of the body-mind that is required to be able to serve these needs. One needs a top-level view to be able to see this and get started with a task that no one is focusing on. The more the body-mind gets trained, than he takes up greater tasks of service that are being unattended. One who is clear leads an impersonal life. It is only after realizing the truth that one can render the best service. If you know that you can render your best service only when you know how to work on the computer, then you would train yourself to be able to effectively use the computer. Similarly, one who wants to be of best service would chose to embrace spirituality so as to realize the truth. Such a person embraces spirituality, not at all because he is unhappy, but because he wants to be of service in the best possible way. This does not mean that those who are unhappy do not get into spirituality. They too must and will embrace spirituality. If someone is not visiting a doctor even after falling sick, then he needs psychiatric counseling! If one is egoistic, one would not go to a place when he is not recognized or praised. If such a person is told that he will never get any credit if he embraces spirituality, he would never go there. In contrast, some people love the truth. Regardless of whether they gets appreciated or not, people who yearn for the truth will say that knowing the exact truth about life is of utmost importance to them. One would say, "Let anyone be praised or credited. But I am interested in realizing the truth. I will continue the quest, since I am more interested in truth than anything else." Their love for the truth, for true freedom is so intense. Worldly material success can be easily attained. But what is the real truth? So many great souls have spoken at length about it. What is it that they had attained, what was their realization? This was the only focus. Whoever may have spoken about the truth is immaterial, but if what was spoken can help in realizing the truth, then it is important. Let the credit go to any religion, it does not matter; we should attain the truth. Be it by reading the Gita, the Quran, or the Bible, be it by following any guru, attain the truth is the only purpose; that alone is of importance. When such intensity arises within someone, he too embraces spirituality, not because he is unhappy or depressed. This notion that only depressed or troubled people take to spirituality is baseless. Those who carry this wrong belief should read or listen to this. Even if one is not depressed or troubled, one can still want to understand the crux of the essential truth, which so many great seers have tirelessly praised, in love of which such wonderful hymns have been sung, about which numerous books have been written, around which so many religions have been established, for which so much packaging has been created.

17. Is God displeased if man does not abide by religion?

A: Regardless of whether one abides by religion or not, if one does not understand God, then words such as 'displeasure' will be used for God. Who is God? Who am I? Till one does not realize this secret, such beliefs will persist. God and displeasure are two opposites. It is like asking whether green color is crooked or straight, whether green color is hot or cold. You would say that if you are analyzing green color this way, it means that you have not understood what green color really means? If God is considered in the right context, then this puzzle is solved. You have already seen that wherever the word 'Dharma' or 'God' is used, due to the existence of two distinct contexts or meanings, it has created confusion. Why would God be displeased at all? It is like saying that water is dry. The very freedom with which man is able to live today is proof that God is not displeased. God has given complete allowance and freedom to man to choose what he wants. Can there be a greater proof of His boundless unconditional love!

18. How to abide by our religion? How to be truly religious?

A: We need to attain Bright understanding. Whatever religion you may follow, be it Hinduism, Islam, Christianity, Sikhism, Buddhism, Jainism, it is important to associate Bright understanding (Tejgyan) with it. Bright understanding is the experiential wisdom that is beyond all dualities such as happiness and sorrow, success and failure, life and death, knowledge and ignorance. It is the thread of understanding that binds all religions together. A doctor who associates Bright understanding will be able to fulfill the purpose of becoming a doctor. With the passage of time, this understanding becomes shrouded. The one who goes beyond both patient and doctor is a Bright doctor – a doctor with Bright understanding. One who does not have Bright understanding will continue to blindly follow rituals, believing that he is abiding by his religion. He will not be able to progress beyond it. So until one attains Bright understanding, one can continue to read religious scriptures. Subsequently, when one attains Bright understanding, he will then realize that he is able to truly read and relate to his religious scripture in the right way. He will find that he is able to understand the essence of the Bible, the Quran, or the Gita. This is possible because he is watching from his essential nature. He is able to experience the Self, the experience of 'beingness' which is being felt not on the body, but due to the presence of the body. When you stabilize in the conviction of this experience which is beyond the body, then you understand the essence of religion and abide by it. You will then be able to understand exactly why realized souls like Jesus or Krishna, Buddha, or Mahavir made those statements that have been noted down in scriptural form. Abiding by your religion will become natural when you associate Bright understanding with it. There is no need to get stuck about the vocabulary used here with words like Bright or Tej. Otherwhise, one may misunderstand that these words are being used to prove the superiority of these words. The essence is the experience of Beingness, which is beyond all words, beyond all concepts. It is important to attain this understanding; from where you obtain this understanding is immaterial.

19. With which religion can the truth be attained?

A: This is similar to the question regarding which the effectiveness of prayer with a particular religion. People believe that truth can be only attained only through a particular religious belief-system, through a particular packaging. If you are considering rituals to be religion, then you can never attain the truth through any religion. By considering the rituals to be religion, people become headstrong and boast about their knowledge of scriptures or rituals. They will be able to recite any verse from the scripture. This has nothing to do with attaining the truth. Until you do not gain conviction in your essential beingness, your true nature, the truth cannot be attained. Therefore you are instructed to be seated in meditation, at least for a short time to begin with, so as to build recognition of your essential nature, the real 'I' that is beyond the body. Once you know the real 'I' within, you know everyone. One method is to try and know everyone in the external world; meet people to observe and introspect upon your own nature. This method is prescribed for those whose mental disposition is extroverted. In contrast, there are those who are focused within. They reach within to discover the true nature. Both methods lead to the same destination. You are instructed to follow both these practices at the same time, so that you can benefit both ways – introspection with the external world as well as meditation in the inner world. You may continue the religious rituals or practices that you have been following earlier; it is not necessary to stop that. It is good if you have a habit of praying every morning as part of certain set rituals. We can convert rituals into an opportunity to go further. With one habit, you can always associate many other reminders. Habits act as anchors that can be used to remember the truth. If no habit (ritual) has been inculcated, then there's nothing to which you can associate reminders. You will remember the truth one day, and forget it the very next day. Children are taught basic alphabet in kindergarten. This becomes useful in later years when he uses the alphabet and associates them with a sequence to build words and sentences. By itself, the alphabet is of no use. It becomes useful only when it is associated for a higher purpose. It is only when the student uses it to construct sentences that he appreciates the knowledge of the alphabet that was imparted in childhood. Similarly, the habit of chanting was imparted to people at the basic level. The real use of chanting comes at an advanced stage when the chanting can be associated with the reminder of the truth. However, if the person never reaches the advanced stage and merely keeps chanting mechanically without knowing the real purpose, then it remains just a ritual. This is a very common mistake. So by understanding this, you can benefit from the habit of rituals that you have gained since childhood and make use of them as opportunity for the real purpose of stringing the reminder of truth with it, without getting stuck in the packaging.

20. Is it necessary to change or convert one's religion in order to attain the truth?

A: To attain the truth, it is important to change yourself. There are people who entice others to convert their religious faith. One may feel that if I am unable to attain the truth by following my existing religious belief-system why not try conversion into some other religious faith. But after converting, the person spends a few more years to understand the new religious belief-system and practices. Changing religions is of no use. You are best placed wherever you are right now. When man himself changes and understands that I was considering my body to be myself. When he changes this thought and start living by being what he truly is, then he attains the truth. Changing religions is like changing cages. Initially one may feel nice about like exploring the new cage. But later, you find it is the same because you have not changed; only the packaging has changed. The better option is to associate understanding of why this variety of religious faiths and rituals were established by realized souls. Man's thinking needs to change. This can be achieved through deep self-introspection. Otherwise, man lives in the delusion by holding onto his limiting beliefs, considering them to be the reality. By holding onto such limiting beliefs, he attracts a limited life. When he is told this, he rejects it as he cannot accept that he is wrong in this life. If he is fed with another belief that this limited life that he is suffering from is due to the effects of a previous life, he chooses to accept that, since he still maintains that he is right in this lifetime.

21. Will I attain truth by abiding by religion, or will I abide by religion when I attain the truth?

A: After realization of the truth, people begin to notice the outward manifestation. The body-mind where truth has been attained serves in various ways. However, due to the focus on the external expression, people wrongly believe the attainment of truth to be the result of such external expression. They put the result before the cause. The general belief is that remembering the truth will lead to attainment of the truth. But, the reality is exactly the opposite – upon attaining the truth, remembrance alone remains. But someone who sees this will believe that constant remembrance can lead to attainment of the truth. So then the realized one helplessly asks people to practice remembrance at least for some time. That which naturally follows after the attainment can be practiced before the attainment. The secondary happening which is the external manifestation can be grasped, but the primary happening, the inner shift in understanding cannot be grasped easily Hence, the secondary aspect is given more importance. People are engaged in various practices to attain the truth without understanding what the essential truth is. These practices are beneficial in a worldly sense, but have nothing to do with the essential truth. The essential truth has to come first. We are not talking about the verbal material truth of the external world here. The verbal truth that this is a boy, or this is a girl, or it is now daytime has nothing to with the essential truth. We are talking about the truth that exists in the background; that which exists behind the stage on which the drama of this world is being played. The individual that does not exist is assuming himself to be separate from totality. This is an illusion. There is no separation; there is only one, the Universal 'I' which is experiencing itself through the medium of this world. When this truth that the individual does not exist becomes not only acceptable but also delightful, when all duality ends, then one is abiding in the truth. After attainment of the truth, all religions and their varied expression come later. So attainment of truth has to come first.

22. Why is a new religion established with every self-realized soul?

A: A new religion does not necessarily get established with every body-mind where self-realization has taken place. This may happen in certain specific contexts at certain places where people are steeped in ignorance. In such contexts, the need arises that people should follow one single tenet to progress life. When each one was worshipping their own deities and following their own individual rituals, guiding everyone towards the truth became difficult. It is easier to guide masses who follow the same idol or school of thought, using the same religious scripture. So in such contexts where the need was felt with a large population, a common religious faith was established to bring all people under a common understanding of the essential truth. But, this does not mean that all self-realized souls need to establish new religions. As you can see today, we are not talking about establishing a new religion; we are working on the thread of understanding that can bind all religions, to create a temple of humanity where the human mind can be focused within, so as to realize the truth. There is no need to convert or change your existing faith. Wherever you are, you only need to add, the understanding of the truth. One can become instrumental for spreading the truth in this manner. Every body-mind is free to choose how to serve or express the truth. There was a need for a new religion in ancient times; now there is no such need. It was possible with certain realized souls; it depends on how trained the body-mind was. Saint Meera would never establish a new religion. Creation happens depending on the body-mind where realization has taken place and the needs of people. Whatever becomes a need gets created. For example, when the world needed the computer, it was invented. Similarly whatever is the need today on earth, creations will happen accordingly. The more trained the body-minds that become instrumental for bringing forth these creations on earth, the more creations earth will witness.

23. Is self-realization or the experience of Self different in different religions?

A: The experience of the Self is the same in all religions. It is well known that the saint Ramakrishna Parmahamsa followed various rituals. But, the reality is that he had already attained the truth. He did not follow rituals in order to attain the truth. He had already attained the truth, and was following various rituals later. One who is established in the experience of the Self can never forget it. One who has attained would say that all the books, the Bible, the Kuran, and Gita would lead to the same experience. Ramakrishna also confirmed the same truth that all books and rituals point to the same underlying experience of the truth. Self-realized souls continue to follow rituals even after self-realization out of love and compassion, so that people around them do not feel hurt. But this led to the belief that those rituals can lead to self-realization. For the one who has realized the truth, the significance of rituals becomes clear. Very often, we follow certain practices only so that our children emulate us. If children need to sit and study for their exams, the parents will also sit beside them with their work, so as to arouse interest in the children. It is not the urgent need of the parents, but they would still sit with their children so as to teach them by example. Similarly, self-realized souls engage in rituals only to teach people around them, arising from happiness and compassion. It is fun for the realized souls. It is not at all an ordeal for them to fast and do penance.

24. Is the expression of every self-realized soul as per their religion? Do all of them propagate their teachings?

A: Where self-realization happens, expression happens naturally and spontaneously, arising from bliss. People who come into the scene later misuse the recorded history of realized souls to prove their point in an attempt to dominate. All the benefits that arise in the form of propagation of teachings are a bonus. The expression by the self-realized soul was never with the purpose of spreading or propagation. Did Buddha ever propagate Buddhism? When Buddha attained nirvana, there was nothing called Buddhism! He was not spreading any religion. He was only conveying the simple truth that there is a way out of unhappiness. People who do not understand this will believe that he propagated Buddhism. Buddha was never interested in spreading Buddhism per se. He was only conveying the truth as a natural expression. The self-realized soul would say, let whatever yields result be used to help people attain the truth. With this intention, if someone uses Hindu aspects to convey the truth as most people who are listening to him follow Hindu traditions, he is not propagating Hinduism. He is only using Hindu tenets as an instrument to convey the essential truth. But people will assume that he is propagating Hinduism. But the one who is explaining the truth does so with the sole intention that people should know their true nature and experience the Self which he is already experiencing. They make use of whatever comes before them as an effective instrument to convey the truth. However, people get stuck with the instrument that was used. Some of the instruments were concepts that were already popular. For example, there is a prevalent belief that this lifetime is determined by actions from a previous lifetime. This belief was used by self-realized souls, not to foster this belief, but to convey the essential truth using this pretext. In certain segments of society, the belief that there is only one birth became popular. Even this belief was used to convey the real truth. If people are convinced about these concepts, then these concepts can be used as instruments only to convey the truth. People were served the truth in their own plates (using their own beliefs). However, the beliefs by themselves were of no real consequence. But then these beliefs became strong. The sole interest of the self-realized soul is to convey the truth in the language that can benefit the audience, so that people can progress from wherever they are towards attaining the truth. If the truth can be conveyed using contemporary language used in films, then so be it. That does not mean that the self-realized soul is promoting films! What the self-realized soul speaks will also depend on the language that the body-mind has learnt. Some people wrongly believe that the one who is self-realized will start speaking in all the languages such as French, German, and Spanish. This is not so. Whatever language the body-mind was trained in will be used for the benefit of the audience. Whatever yields result will be used to convey the truth. The sole intention is that people should abide in their true nature. People should dwell in love, joy, and peace.

25. Which religion does Tej Gyan Foundation believe in? Is it creating a new religion?

A: Tejgyan follows the religion of Love, Joy, and Peace! If you wish to add any further words that represent divine qualities, you may. But the key message is that Tej Gyan Foundation intends to be the back-office for every religion. The back-office supports the needs of people who keep calling them for help. The clear message is that people are free to follow whatever they are pursuing today. There is no compulsion to follow Tejgyan. Whatever you pursue is useful; do follow it. But, the back-office also needs to clearly tell people where they can reach with whatever they are pursuing. If they are following a particular meditation technique, then they need to be told how far they can progress with that technique. But if you progress till that point and find that you still want to go further, then you will need to add the following things into your practice. It should be crystal clear to people. Wherever you want to go is good. There is still more that can be attained. People need to be guided clearly and sincerely. If their aim is as per whatever they are pursuing, then they do not need any inputs from Tej Gyan Foundation. They can continue practicing whatever they are doing today. But if you feel like progressing further, you are free to contact us at your convenience; you will be supplied with all the necessary assistance and guidance to help you further in your journey. There is no need for a new religion; rather there is the need for a thread to bind all religions together. When there is no need for a separate religion, then that role will no longer exist. One can focus on creating new means that can help derive benefits from what already exists. If a person shops every day, then when is he going to use whatever he has purchased? There's no point in shopping something new every day, without using what is already shopped. So the need is to train people on properly using whatever they have already purchased. People need to be trained to make use of their religion more effectively so as to attain the truth.

26. Do we need to renounce our religion after associating with Tej Gyan Foundation?

A: You will renounce dharma (non-spiritual living). In other words, you will have to renounce whatever is apart from your true nature. And the renunciation will be effortless. That which is not your true nature will automatically drop off when you are connected here. So if dharma is understood to be one's true nature, then this question is answered. If one assumes one's religion to be the packaging, then the question will still remain, whether we will have to cast away something in order to embrace some new teachings etc. You have to change yourself; merely changing external rituals will not lead you anywhere. Dharma refers to qualitics that are not aligning with your true nature. Anger is not your natural quality; love is. Whatever is anti-love will automatically be renounced when you are associated here, because you would never want to trouble yourself. By being angry, one only punishes oneself. One who is truly happy and loves himself will never want to trouble himself by being angry.

CHAPTER 17

To give form to God is an essential mistake,
The assuming of a form by God is a necessity.
The world is a form, which is a need of the formless.
The world is a mirror, which is a face of the formless.

Significance of Worship of Various Deities

Devotion by contemplating the qualities of God

Let us understand seven prominent forms of God that are commonly worshipped in the Indian context. These forms are symbolic representations that help in understanding the true nature of God.

1. GANESHA

Parvati (God in action) gave birth to Ganesha from the dirt on her body. This indicates the birth of the first man, the first wonder. Ganesha symbolizes the Guru who works as a bridge between the devotee and God.

The parts depicted in the form of Ganesha symbolize the following:

Head of an elephant Wide forehead – a sharp intellect and Understanding.

Big ears Receptivity for the truth – It is necessary to listen before attaining understanding.

Small eyes Concentration – the power of

	concentration is necessary in order to keep the mind focused on the truth.
Long Trunk	In order to explore any subject and catch all its subtle nuances, one must delve deep into the subject. Ganesha can lift a heavy rock or even a tiny needle with his trunk. This means that while the grosser aspects of truth are understood, one should be able to grasp even the subtle aspects.
Wives – Riddhi, Siddhi	On the path to self-realization, no matter how much success one might have attained, one should not forget the truth. Ganesha is always egoless, in spite of having Riddhi and Siddhi (prosperity and power) beside him as his wives.
Two tusks - one broken	Symbolizes being balanced in all states of duality that one comes across. States of duality imply the experience of opposites such as joy-sorrow, honor-insult, hot-cold, etc. It symbolizes the attainment of knowledge that is beyond duality. To convey the message of 'liberation from duality', one of the tusks shown as being broken. Tejgyan (Bright knowledge which is beyond knowledge and ignorance) and Tej Anand (Bright happiness which is beyond joy and sorrow) can only be attained by going beyond duality.
Rat	The rat symbolizes greed, lust and desires. Its hunger is never satiated. It always burrows into something, even needlessly. It is just like our contrast mind that keeps

somersaulting on every thought it receives. The rat accumulates more food than its real need in its burrow. Lord Ganesha has attained victory over greed and lust. He has kept the rat under control. Hence he rides the rat.

If you too acquire all these qualities and move towards self-realization, then you will have become a true devotee of Lord Ganesha. You will have benefited from the form of Ganesha.

2. ARDHANARESHWARI (HALF MAN, HALF WOMAN) (COMBINATION OF LORD SHIVA AND GODDESS PARVATI)

Shiva Other names – Shankara, Bholenath, Neelkantha, Shambu, Nataraja.The state that existed when the world had not been created.Everything has been created from the power of Shiva. Shiva is the essence of every living being. Without the presence of Shiva, a body is just a corpse.

Parvati Other names – Maya, Parameshwari, Shakti (Shiva's Power), Nature, Uma. Maya (Illusion) – It appears that Shiva is lost because of this. The way to self-realization involves the clearing *of* maya.

Serpent Symbolizes death. Death is wrapped around the neck of Shiva and yet he is calm. This indicates victory over death.

Moon The moon symbolizes coolness and calm. Shiva wears the moon over his head which indicates a cool head (a thoughtless state).

Ganges The River Ganges is depicted as if it is flowing from the hair locks of Lord Shiva. This symbolizes pure knowledge of the Self. King Bhagirath prayed to Lord Shiva to contain the immense flow of the Ganges (knowledge). Only the one who has his third eye (divine vision) open can contain the flow of the knowledge of truth.

Third eye Divine vision – When one goes beyond duality, beyond being a recluse or being a man of the world, beyond bondage and freedom, beyond honor and humiliation, it can be said that the third eye has opened.

Nandi, the Bull This symbolizes the mind. The bull is depicted as being seated outside the temple facing Shiva. This means that the mind should always remain focused inwards. Such a mind does not get stuck to thoughts of the external world. When the mind is focused within, it is in a temple.

Half open eyes Depicts the state of meditation. Even while the attention is focused outside, it is still established in the experience of Self.

Trishul Trident – symbolizes the body, mind, and intellect. It serves as an instrument to destroy the ego.

Ardhanareshwari

The form comprising half Shiva and half Parvati. Shiva (Self) and Shakti (power) are not two different entities; they are two states of the same entity. These two names have been given only to understand the two states.

3. VISHNU

Vishnu Other names – Narayana, Satyanarayana, Hari. The state of rest of God before the world was formed. The protector. The world is looked after by Vishnu. Vishnu is the consciousness within us due to which we are alive.

Laxmi Other names – Narayani, Maya, Wealth.The state when God came into action.

The world The manifest form of God, the mirror for God to experience himself

Ocean The mind filled with thoughts, the mind with the waves of thoughts.

Ocean of milk *Satvik* mind, pure balanced mind. Vishnu resides in the minds of those, who do not have the qualities of *tamas* or rajas.

King of serpents (multi-headed serpent)

The ego with its many desires (heads) which is focused on Lord Vishnu alone. Only by looking inwards can one attain victory over ego and desires.

Yogic state of rest

Lord Vishnu is in the *Turiya* state. He is established in the experience of being. This state depicts the state of a person who has attained self-realization. Even with Laxmi (wealth) at his feet, he does not waver from his true nature and remains established in it. Those who want to attain Vishnu should not get caught up in the words of Laxmi (also the symbol of *maya* or delusion).

Blue complexion

Symbolizes the sky – omnipresent, all-pervading.

Crown Symbolizes ruling the whole world.

Conch Shell Vishnu holds this in one hand. This symbolizes the instrument to spread the sound of truth all over the world.

Lotus Vishnu is holding a lotus in one hand. This symbolizes truth – the whole and sole purpose of life.

Mace In the third hand is the mace. It is the weapon used to keep the ego under control on the path to self-realization.

Sudarshan Chakra

(a spiked discus, Lord Vishnu's weapon) This is held on the index finger of his fourth hand. It is the weapon used to cut through any hurdle. A weapon of self-defense (understanding) used to prevail over the vices of the mind.

The symbolism of Vishnu and Laxmi indicates how the world was formed, how everything is pervaded by Vishnu, and how one can attain self-realization.

4. SHIVALINGA: DEPICTION OF THE FORMLESS SHIVA

Shakti (Power) God in action – the formation of the world.

Shiva God at rest – God in the formless state. The Shivalinga is a depiction of this state.

Linga The lower half of the idol that is buried underground depicts Shiva.The upper half of the idol that protrudes above the ground depicts the power of Shiva – the world.

Round-shape Depicts the absolute – that which has neither a beginning nor an end. This is a quality of God – boundlessness

Om Omkar – the inner voice.

The Shivalinga has been made to dispel the notion of shape and form and evoke the feeling of nothingness.

5. TRINITY (GOD)

Brahma The creator(G = Generator)

Vishnu The protector (O = Operator)

Mahesha The destroyer (D = Destroyer)

In truth these are not three, but one. The Trinity depicts different functions of the same power.

6. MOTHER KALI

Just as the form of man, the form of a woman has also been used to depict certain attributes of God.

Kali The power of God, the manifest form of God.

Shiva The depiction of Lord Shiva under the feet of Mother Kali indicates that the origin of all the powers is Shiva alone, which is unseen and present within all of us.

Black color This symbolizes darkness and ignorance. It is due to the power of Kali that man is caught up in the ignorance of beliefs. Till the time Mother Kali (maya – illusion) does not will so, one cannot come out of this darkness. Just as a hypnotist can bring someone out of his hypnotic spell only when he wishes to.

Navaratra (Nine Nights)

The symbolic period on the path to self-realization. Here three Goddesses are worshiped for three nights each – Durga, Saraswati and Kali.

Garland of severed heads

The death of desires, cravings and ego.

Sword Weapon to cut the ego, destroy the contrast mind.

Skull and outstretched tongue

The depiction that not a single drop of blood should spill on the ground. This indicates that no new desires should arise in the mind. Otherwise it has been seen that no sooner a desire dies down, a new one takes its place.

Shumbha - Nishumbha

Two powerful demons symbolizing attachment and aversion, slain by Goddess Kali.When, whatever the mind wants and whatever the mind resists, are both killed, the entire army of demons is slain.

CHAPTER 18

The formless alone is the form of God.
Attribute-less is the attribute of God.
The mind is the spectacles of God.
The spectacles can never see the eye.
Hence, the mind can never know God.
God reveals Himself only when the 'no-mind'

Seeking Truth in Idols

The Secrets of Idol Worship

Should one worship idols at all? If we do worship idols, then how should we benefit from it?

Guru Nanak has stated two drawbacks about idol worship. He attempted to illustrate these to people through examples.

At a pilgrimage, some people were standing and offering water to the sun. When Guru Nanak saw this he turned his back to the sun and began to sprinkle water into the sky. People standing around him pointed out that the sun is towards the east and he is offering water in the opposite direction. Guru Nanak said, 'But I am watering my fields.' Hearing this, the people laughed at him and said, 'How can the water reach the fields from here.' He replied, 'If your water can reach the sun, then my fields are closer. The water can surely reach there.' Guru Nanak's had a unique way of conveying the truth.

Even today, people need guides like Guru Nanak. The drawbacks he stated were:

1. You think the all-pervasive God to be as tiny as the idol. When someone steals the idol, you become enraged with the thought that your God has been stolen. This drawback can be eliminated through Bright understanding.
2. You lock up the idol in the temple and commit sin all day, believing yourself to be out of God's sight. But when you understand God to be formless, all-pervasive, and all-knowing, you will realize that you can never sin by being out of his sight.

The use of idol worship for attaining self-realization

Whenever you solve an arithmetic problem of an unknown variable, you begin by naming the unknown variable as 'x' or by assuming a value for it, say '100'. You are then able to find the answer with the help of this assumed name or assumed value. We can apply the same principle to the question, 'Should we perform idol worship?'

A devotee may assume the invisible God to be in the idol, not forgetting the reality that the idol is only a placeholder. He can then attain the truth in the same manner as the student of mathematics resolves the unknown quantity by making use of the variable or placeholder - 'x'. The 'x' is merely instrumental in finding the unknown value. After the unknown value is found, the imagined or assumed 'x' automatically loses significance and does not become an obstacle. In the same manner, idols too should aid us in finding the ultimate truth and should not become the cause of hatred, violence or superstition. A devotee knows, "If God is everywhere, then why not in idols too?!"

Idols and Saints

Meera realized the truth	- She used to worship the idol of Lord Krishna.
Guru Nanak realized the truth	- He worshiped the formless.

Ramakrishna realized the truth	- He worshiped the idol of Mother Kali.
Buddha realized the truth	- He explained the qualities of meditation and nothingness.
You too realize the truth	- Then you will allow divine expression to happen through you.
	Whether idol worship happens through you or not would be irrelevant, as you would always remain in divine bliss.

One should not remain stuck with idols, but at the same time one shouldn't ignore their significance either. How can the importance of an idol be understood? Swami Vivekanand has illustrated this in a very different way.

Once, when Swami Vivekananda was a guest in a royal palace, the king asked him a question in the presence of his courtiers, 'I have no faith in idol-worship. I do not believe in a God made of metal, clay or paper. Would this lack of faith be detrimental for me? Will I be punished for this after my death?' Vivekananda replied, 'Why should you be punished? Worship according to your own belief and you will not be punished.' Hearing this, the courtiers were surprised. They began gossiping, 'Swami himself goes to the temple to bow in prayer, and he is now saying that the king will not be punished!' The king countered him with another question. 'Does this mean that one should not practice idol worship?' Swami Vivekanand pointed at the king's portrait that was hanging on the wall and said, 'Get the portrait off the wall.' The portrait was taken off the wall placed in front him. The Swami said, 'Now spit on it.' The king was aghast at what he had heard. The Swami then asked everyone who was present, 'Can any of you come forward and spit on the portrait?' None came forward.

The Swami then explained to the king, 'You are not in this idol, and yet, neither you nor your courtiers could come forward and spit on it. Similarly, as you said, there is no God in the idol made of metal, clay or paper. But the idols would not have been made without God. The idol is a symbolic representation through which divine qualities are portrayed and remembered. Do you go in front of an idol and say, 'O metal! I am offering you this garland of flowers. O paper! I am bowing down to you in all humility.' You never say so. Similarly people know that you are not in this portrait. It does not move around like you do. Even so, nobody was willing to spit on it. This is because they all felt your presence in it. In the idol, people do not see metal; instead they feel the presence of god. This feeling alone gives them results.

Some people worship idols with blind faith in ignorance. Others show off their knowledge by opposing at idol worship. Both have incomplete knowledge. The quest for truth can begin with form and end in the formless.

The New Temple of God

Let us understand a new symbolism that captures the essence of the truth and therefore can serve as a temple in today's context.

There is a unique fan which has just one blade. A thin pipe is attached to the fan along its blade and it is filled with soap solution. As soon as the fan begins to rotate, the soap solution comes out in the form of bubbles. The soap bubbles start floating in the breeze generated by the fan. Each bubble assumes itself to be separate from the others. It begins to feel that it is moving from one place to another on its own accord. The individualistic ego is born in the bubble. By eliminating this ego, it is possible to realize God (the stationary state of the fan represents the original state of God).

In this example there are three states:

1. The fan is stationary – God's formless state
This is the state when the world was not created. This is the state of God at Rest (Shiva, Brahma, Vishnu are names that represent this state.)

2. The fan begins to rotate – The state of forms of God
This is the state where the world has been created. This is God in Action. (Laxmi, Parvati, Saraswati, Shakti are names for this state.)

3. The soap water takes the form of double-bubbles
There is air within as well as outside the bubbles. This is that state of God where along with the creation of the world, the ego got created in man.

Stationary Fan	God at rest (action-less state)
Rotating Fan	God in expression (State of action)
Double-bubble	Human body-mind, the outer gross body and the inner subtle body.
Air	The power of God which is outside us as well as within us. We are in God and God is in us.

All the idols of God explained in the previous chapters, unravel the secret illustrated above. 'The single-bladed fan' is the new form of God in today's language. No one can practice business-like devotion with this form. Otherwise, by giving God the form of man, people have been getting their own wishes fulfilled all the time. This form of God enables people to recognize God's true identity. 330 million deities have been created in India to depict this secret. We need to contemplate deeply on this analogy of the single-bladed fan.

SINGLE-BLADED FAN – THE SECRET OF GOD'S IDOL

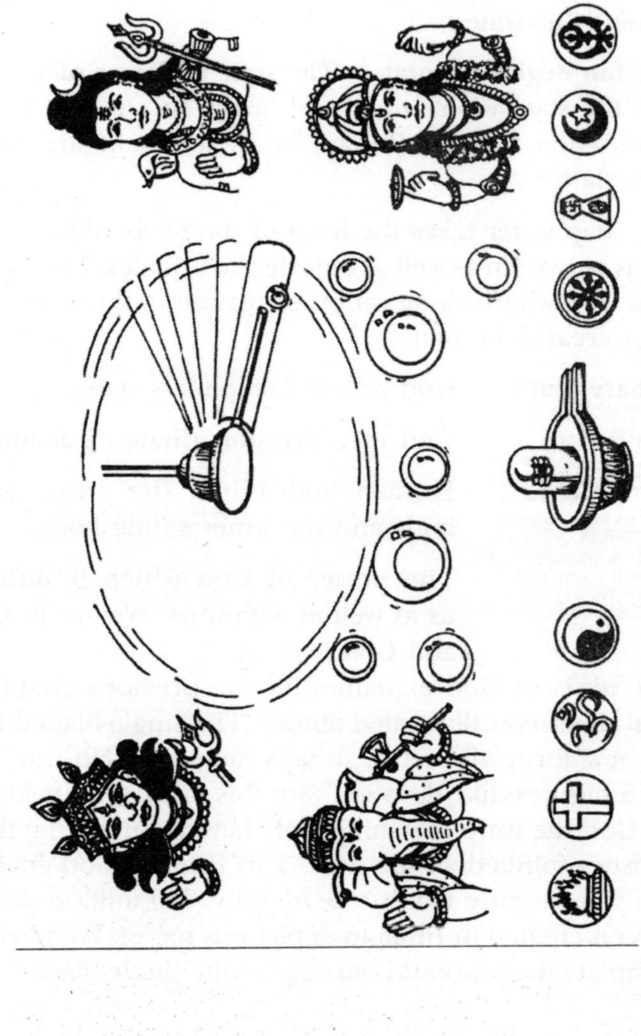

THE NEW TEMPLE OF GOD TODAY

The notions and imaginations about God

A survey was conducted on many aspects related to God. The purpose was to know the various prevalent schools of thought that people pursue. Do they believe in God or not? How much importance have they given to the attainment of God? In what form do they imagine God? Will the attainment of God take place in this birth?

A survey of this is presented below. The question that was put up was: 'How do you perceive God?'

Cannot say	15%
Shiva, Krishna, Mother Goddess, Ram, Buddha, Jesus (The images that are shown on the television)	10%
God is a Soul, Formless (Attribute-less)	6.5%
If one obtains joys, peace and contentment then one has attained God	6.5%
Power, Light, Sound, Kundalini, Elixir of life	3%
God meets us in our dreams	3%
God meets us in the form of the Guru	3%
He can be seen in all forms	4%
God has already been attained	4%
God is attained in the form of death, in a fearsome form, etc.	16%

From the survey we find that more people believe that God can be attained (73%). But these beliefs and notions pertaining to God that have been deeply engrained in human psyche are hurdles in the supreme quest. Dispel all false notions and ignorance by deeply contemplating on the questions pertaining to God presented in this book.

BOOKS OF RELATED INTEREST

HOW I FOUND GOD—*Yogi M.K. Spencer*

This is a rare and unique book on spirituality. It contains the thrilling experiences of the author, Yogi M.K. Spencer. His only desire in life was to see God face to face. For this he was imparted spiritual training first by Rishi Ram Ram and thereafter, by God himself assuming the form of Shri Shirdi Sai Baba.

ISBN: 978-81-7822-352-0

INDIAN PHILOSOPHY A-Z
—*Christopher Bartley*

This alphabetical handbook defines and explains key concepts in classical Indian philosophy, identifies controversial issues, describes major traditions of thought, and locates influential thinkers in their intellectual and religious contexts. They introduce the central concepts of the various branches of philosophy written by established philosophers, covering both traditional and contemporary terminology.

ISBN: 978-81-7822-313-1

THE MEDITATION HANDBOOK: Meditations to Make Our Life Happy and Meaningful—*Geshe Kelsang Gyatso*

This book makes you aware and deepens your insight about—What is meditation and how does it work? How to integrate meditation into our daily life. How to find lasting peace and happiness through meditation.

ISBN: 978-81-7822-066-6

MEDITATIONS FOR PEOPLE IN CHARGE

—Paul Brunton

If your authority touches lives or influences minds—or if you're close to someone whose does—this book is a great gift. It's full of accessible, handy, and inspiring wisdom for *parents, teachers, business executives, political administrators, leaders of organizations, doctors, lawyers, religious leaders and counselors, military leaders* and anyone else who wants (or needs) to keep in mind the ultimate happiness of everyone affected by his or her decisions.

ISBN: 978-81-7822-345-2

MEDITATIONS FOR PEOPLE IN CRISIS

—Paul Brunton

Considering the being itself as the centre of happiness, the author describes the stages of awakening that pave the way to fulfilment. He urges the troubled to shed off their gravest inhibitions and graciously acknowledge the self. Only we can attempt an opening to our hearts and mind. For those in Crisis or with someone close in turbulent times—help is at hand.

ISBN: 978-81-7822-341-4

THE QUEST (The Notebooks of Paul Brunton Vol.2)—*Paul Brunton*

This second volume in *The Notebooks of Paul Brunton* gives timely, candid, immediately useful advice about the promises and pitfalls of spiritual seeking. Drawing creatively and in a thoroughly unique fashion upon philosophical insights of both East and West, Dr. Brunton shows clearly and simply how the daily experiences and difficulties of modern living can be successfully transformed into meaningful steps on the timeless search for self-knowledge.

ISBN: 978-81-7822-347-6

PRACTICES FOR THE QUEST: Relax and Retreat (The Notebooks of Paul Brunton Vol.3)—*Paul Brunton*

Practices for the Quest, goes directly to the heart of exercise, techniques, and mental attitudes useful at various stages of spiritual self-discovery and self-development. It explains what qualities must be developed, how they can be developed, and how their development will be tested and proved by life itself.

ISBN: 978-81-7822-368-1

PATHWAYS TO HIGHER CONSCIOUSNESS: The Master Game
—*Robert S. de Ropp*

The book is a clear and concise set of formulae for achieving a higher state of consciousness and gradation of reason. De Ropp outlines the field of battle, and shows how an individual, armed with deep understanding, discipline and real necessity, can wage his or her own personal war against sleep.

ISBN: 978-81-7822-369-8

ROADSIGNS ON THE SPIRITUAL PATH: Living at the Heart of Paradox
—*Philip Goldberg*

This is one of the wisest books to appear in recent years about the perils and promises that are routinely encountered by all spiritual seekers. At a time in history when people are desperately grasping for security and certainty, Roadsigns is an invaluable contribution from a very wise spiritual teacher.

ISBN: 978-81-7822-342-1